LIMITLESS

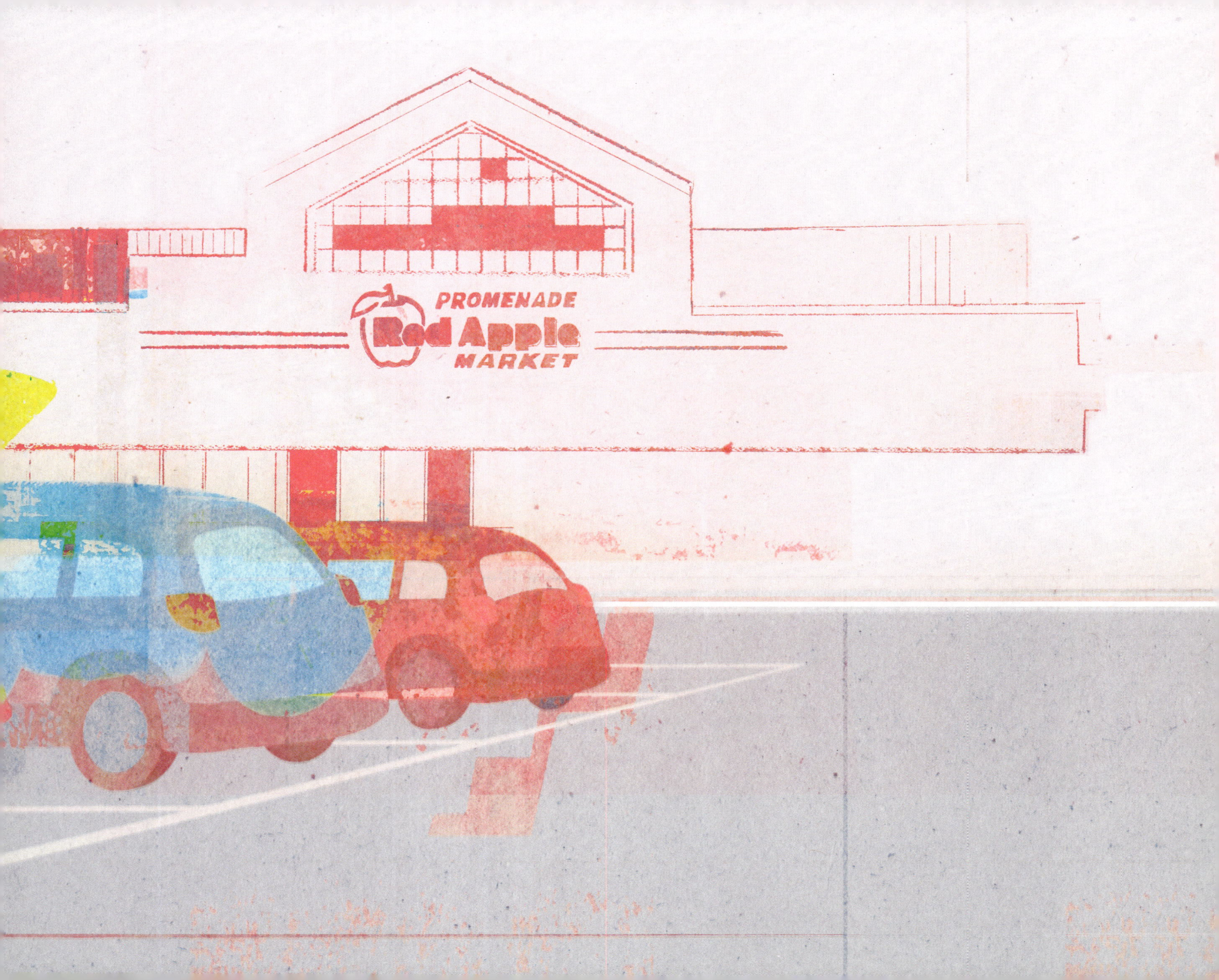
PROMENADE
Red Apple
MARKET

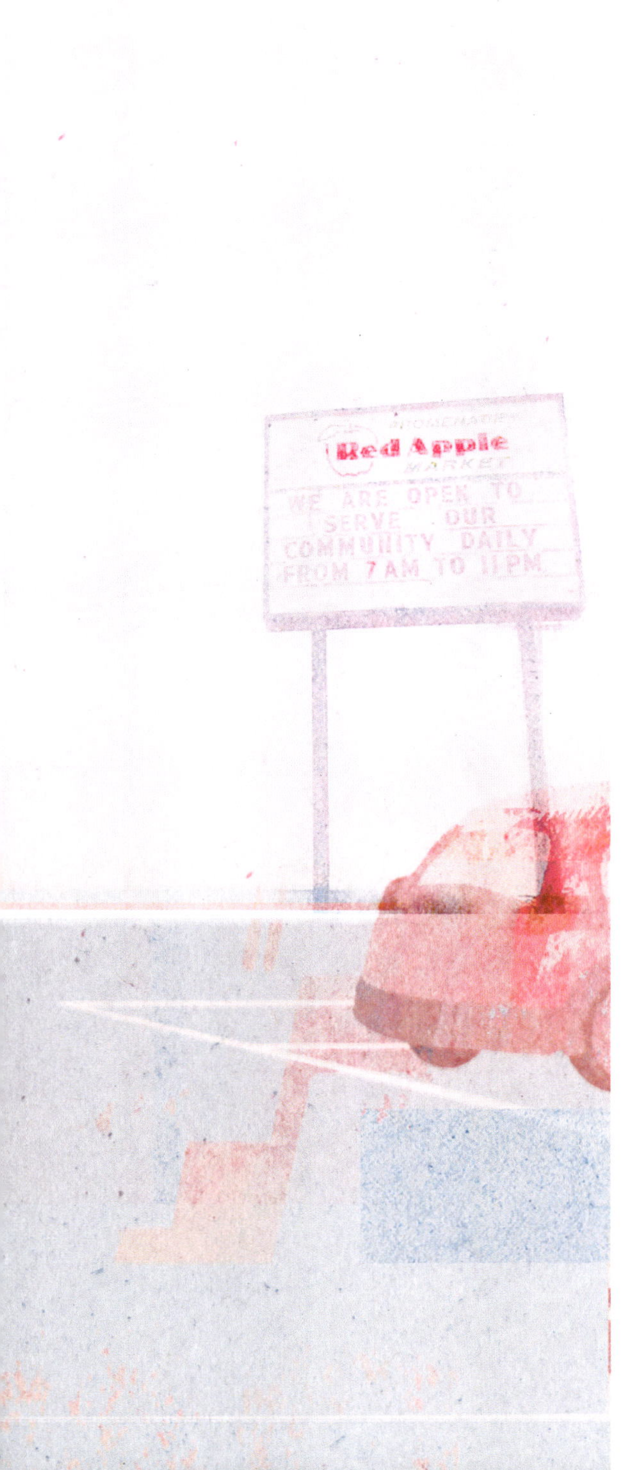

LIMITLESS

STORIES FROM THE NEIGHBORHOOD THAT SHAPED SEATTLE

The Shelf Life
Community
Story Project

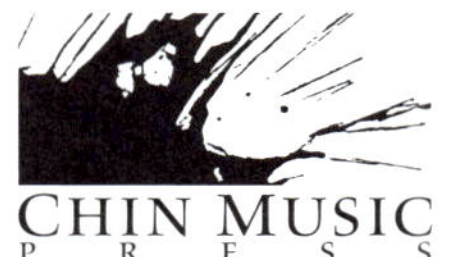

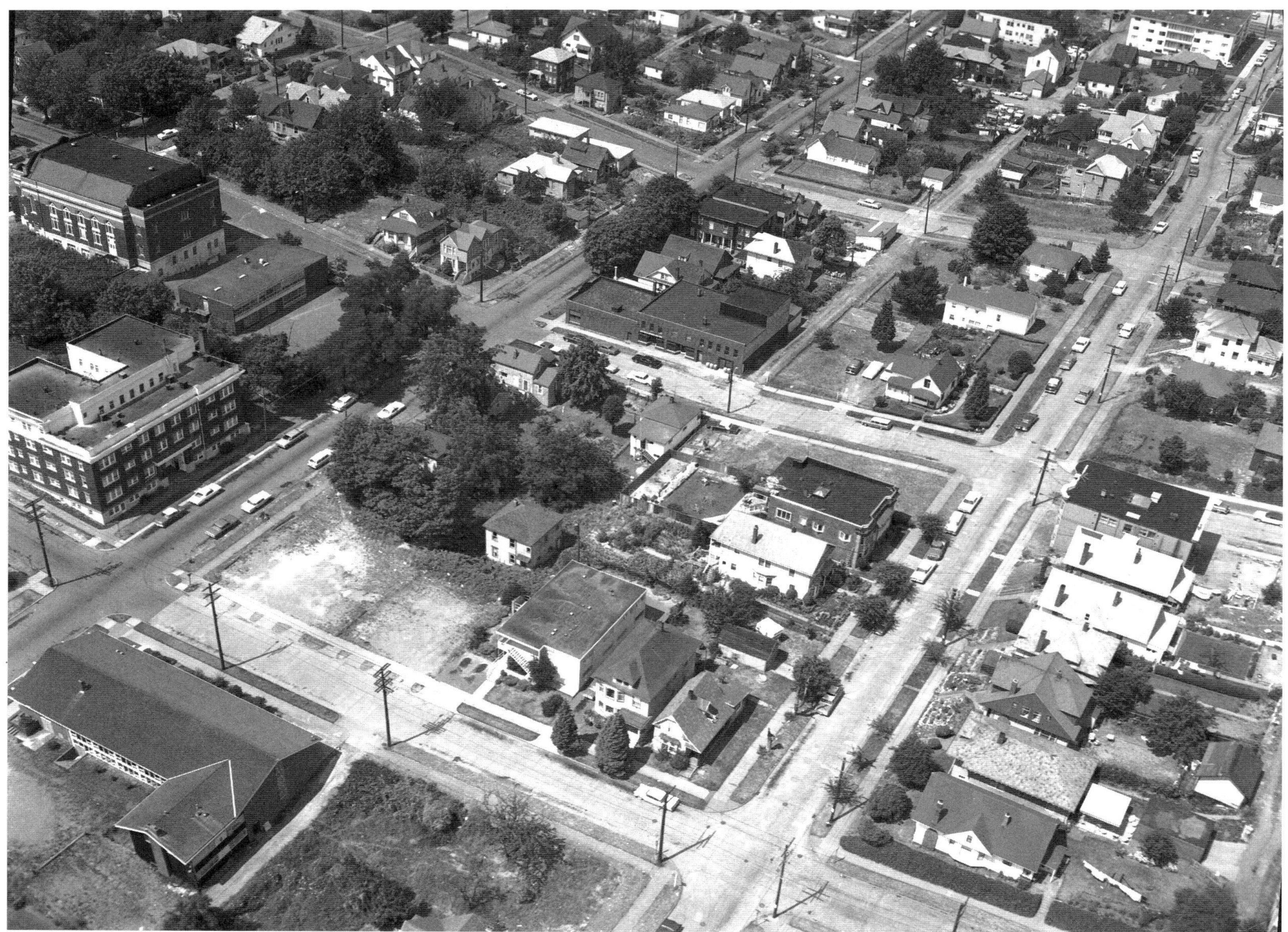

TABLE OF CONTENTS

INTRODUCTION JILL FREIDBERG

In 2016, I unlocked the door to an empty storefront that had previously housed a Subway sandwich shop. It had that clingy smell attributed to Subway "bread." The color palette was mostly "Insurrectionist Gold," which is the actual name assigned to that brownish yellow. The property owner was allowing me to use the space for free.

More importantly, this storefront was next door to the Red Apple grocery store, in the Promenade 23 shopping mall; a single story, '80s era strip mall with an oversized parking lot, an Army recruiting office, and a barber shop. The Red Apple was a community center masquerading as a grocery store; an anchor for residents of the historically-redlined Central District; a place where customers could dance in the aisles to R&B, disco, and soul while shopping for smoked turkey tails and peach cobbler; a business where the manager, who was also a pastor, gladly welcomed regular customers into his office for prayer.

And, it was slated for demolition.

I was a white lady living in a historically-Black, rapidly-gentrifying neighborhood. My favorite grocery store, the Red Apple, seemed to encapsulate all that was being lost as the neighborhood filled up with market-rate townhomes and round-the-clock Amazon deliveries. Carving out a space to record and share the stories of the people who shopped and worked at the Red Apple seemed like as good a way as any to push back against all that loss and the narratives of erasure that accompanied it. It was never just about preservation, locking something away for the future; it was about using the stories of a neighborhood to shift the direction our city was headed.

That's how Shelf Life began. A handful of folks recording stories inside an old Subway sandwich shop. Neighbors would peek their heads in the door, and if they had the time and interest, they'd sit down for a few minutes, or a couple of hours, and let us record their stories. It wasn't long before we figuratively and literally followed people out of the Red Apple and into the neighborhood. Shelf Life became a

neighborhood story project not just a Red Apple
story project.

In that first year, we recorded at least seventy-five
interviews, all of them with people whose roots ran
deep in the Central District. They ranged in age from
twenty-one to ninety-five. These were people who
had been born, raised, taught, fed, loved, inspired,
employed, and protected by the parents and grandparents and aunties of everyone who was told they
couldn't live anywhere else in Seattle. These were the
people who created and innovated and resisted and
celebrated in ways that shaped this city.

The collective of people who built and sustained Shelf
Life, who believed in the project enough to teach a
workshop, or record some stories, or paint a wall,
grew in an organic, word-of-mouth kind of way.
In no particular order, those people were Kristen
Ramirez, Florangela Davila, Dacia Saenz, Sandy Cioffi,
Gretchen Burger, Domonique Meeks, Chieko Phillips,
Leilani Lewis, Stephanie Johnson-Toliver, Henry Luke,
Mayowa Aina, Rachel Kessler, Luzviminda Carpenter,
Luvetra Miles, Lila Lakehart, Carina del Rosario, Inye
Wokoma, Jonathan Cunningham, Karen Toering,
Fidelma McGinn, Sara Post, Allison Bailey, Cristi
Cantrell, Annie Bateman, and Marie Kidhe.

After the Promenade 23 was demolished, others came on
board for the work of sharing the stories we had recorded.
The Shelf Life family grew to include Bubba Jones,
Elisheba Johnson, Wa Na Wari, Ariel Paine, and others.

The stories we recorded have gone out into the world
via podcasts, community radio, walking tours and
more. But I always wanted to see them in a book;
something tangible during a time when everything
feels so intangible. Of course these stories needed to
be wrapped up in the traditions of creativity and artistic brilliance that this neighborhood has always fostered. Artists Damon Brown, Inye Wokoma, Jite Agbro,
Romson Bustillo, Erin Shigaki, Chi Moscou-Jackson,
and Bonnie Hopper all grew up in the Central District.
It shaped them as humans and as artists.

All of this was made possible by everyone mentioned
here, everyone who shared their stories, King County
4Culture, and the City of Seattle Office of Arts and
Culture. Northwest Film Forum has been Shelf Life's
fiscal sponsor since the beginning, a process made so
much easier by the irreplaceable Christopher Day.

One person who never saw the inside of the Shelf Life
space but who, nevertheless, had a hand in shaping
its vision is Rahwa Habte. Rahwa, and her restaurant
Hidmo, are in the DNA of Shelf Life. Hidmo was the
first place, in this city, where I witnessed the use of
art and stories to build collective power. I don't think
any of this would have happened were it not for those
lazy afternoons and crowded, delicious nights of good
food, good music, and good people, on the corner of
20th and Jackson.

Thank you. Thank you. Thank you.

FOREWORD INYE WOKOMA

Behind the Blue Curtain...
Beyond the Blue Curtain

When I was a child we lived in the Mount Baker neighborhood of Seattle, on the eastern slope of the hill, looking east towards the Cascade Mountains. I had a view of Lake Washington and the Cascades from my bedroom. Being the introverted, bookish, daydreamy boy that I was, I would spend hours gazing eastward at the mountains.

I was born in 1969. I came of age in the years just following the era of the Civil Rights and Black Power movements. Because nearly every adult in my life was deeply involved in community activism or institution building, I was acutely aware of the politics of Blackness. This hyper-awareness made me keen to imagine what daily Black life was like in the cities I saw on TV and in the movies: New York, Chicago, Atlanta, Memphis, Detroit.

It was in my long hours reading and daydreaming in my bedroom that the images of Black people in these cities swirled with the view outside my window. I would frequently imagine transporting myself by flight over the mountains and into the teeming ocean of Black life that was the rest of America. I was taken by these flights of fancy because, by comparison to my imagined Black America beyond the Cascades, Black Seattle felt small, quiet, isolated, provincial. Tucked away up here in the Pacific Northwest, Seattle was indeed separated by geography from most of Black America. It was not all my imagination. For me the Cascade Mountain Range was a blue curtain, a boundary I was trapped behind. A borderland beyond which was the fulfillment of everything I longed to be a part of.

In retrospect this longing was born of youthful restlessness and folly. The stories in this volume illustrate just how rich, complex, and vibrant Black life was in twentieth-century Seattle. If one were not careful, the stories of newcomers virtually being plucked off the streets and placed in safe comfortable housing might have you place them in Anytown, Mississippi, or booming postwar Michigan. Unlike the angst-fueled longing of my young imagination, Black Seattle was much like any other Black American migratory outpost, full of people who knew what it meant to come from people, and so would open their arms to new people who needed a warm, soft landing.

Yes, Black Seattle is tucked away, far and apart from the connected cities of the Midwest, South, and East. But contrary to how it may have sometimes felt, we lost no essence of ourselves because of it. Here, behind the blue curtain, we were waiting for newcomers to discover us, and discover this place as a new home.

INYE WOKOMA
Blue Curtain—Trouble the Waters

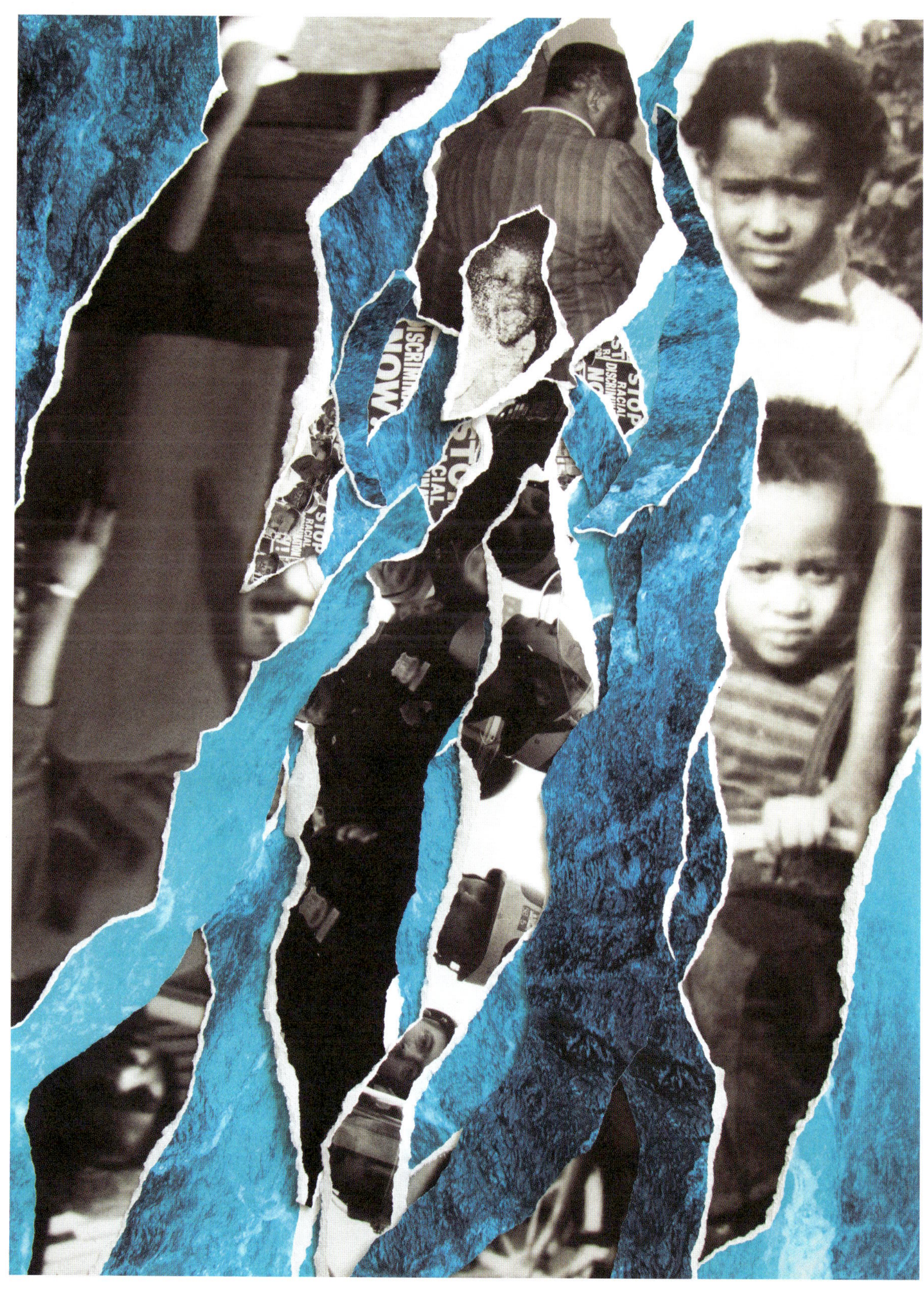
STOP
RACIAL
DISCRIMINATION
NOW

ONE
MIGRATION AND ARRIVAL

i ran

behind the

tall blue

curtain

and found

you

building a fire

for me

you ran

behind the

tall blue

curtain

and found

me

stoking the fire

for you

Inye Wokoma

MY NAME IS

Lottie Cross, and I was born in Oak Ridge, Louisiana. I'm the eighth child of twelve kids, ten girls and two boys.

My mother and father were sharecroppers, down in Louisiana. One year, on the last day of school, we were all dressed to go to school. This man at the plantation that we stayed on comes up and says, "They can't go to school until they pick that cotton." So, I'm thinking, "This the last day of school. We going to school today." But my mother says, "Lottie, they're gonna move us out of this old raggedy house if you don't go out there and pick the cotton. If you all go out there and pick the cotton you might get an hour or two of school in."

I can't remember nobody else being so pissed as I was. We missed school. We missed the last day of school. So as soon as I was old enough, I didn't want to do all that stuff anymore.

My boyfriend moved to Seattle, and my mother said, "Lottie, you need to go and marry him,

he's a good boy." So I told him that whenever he got a job and a place to stay ('cause I wouldn't stay with in-laws) that I would come. I was trying to get rid of him! But seven months later he called me. He had a job, and he had a place for us to stay so...three days and three nights on the train. I wouldn't fly. I was afraid to fly. I was so country.

When I got here, it was a real culture shock. People didn't speak. You know, down in the South, we speak to everybody. Just speak. But I finally got used to it. I made them speak.

I was so lonely up here, even being married. I called my sister, she was getting out of high school, and I said, "I tell you what, you need to come up here and live with me. I can't stand it up here by myself."

So she caught the train and she's been with me ever since.

BONNIE HOPPER
Lottie Cross

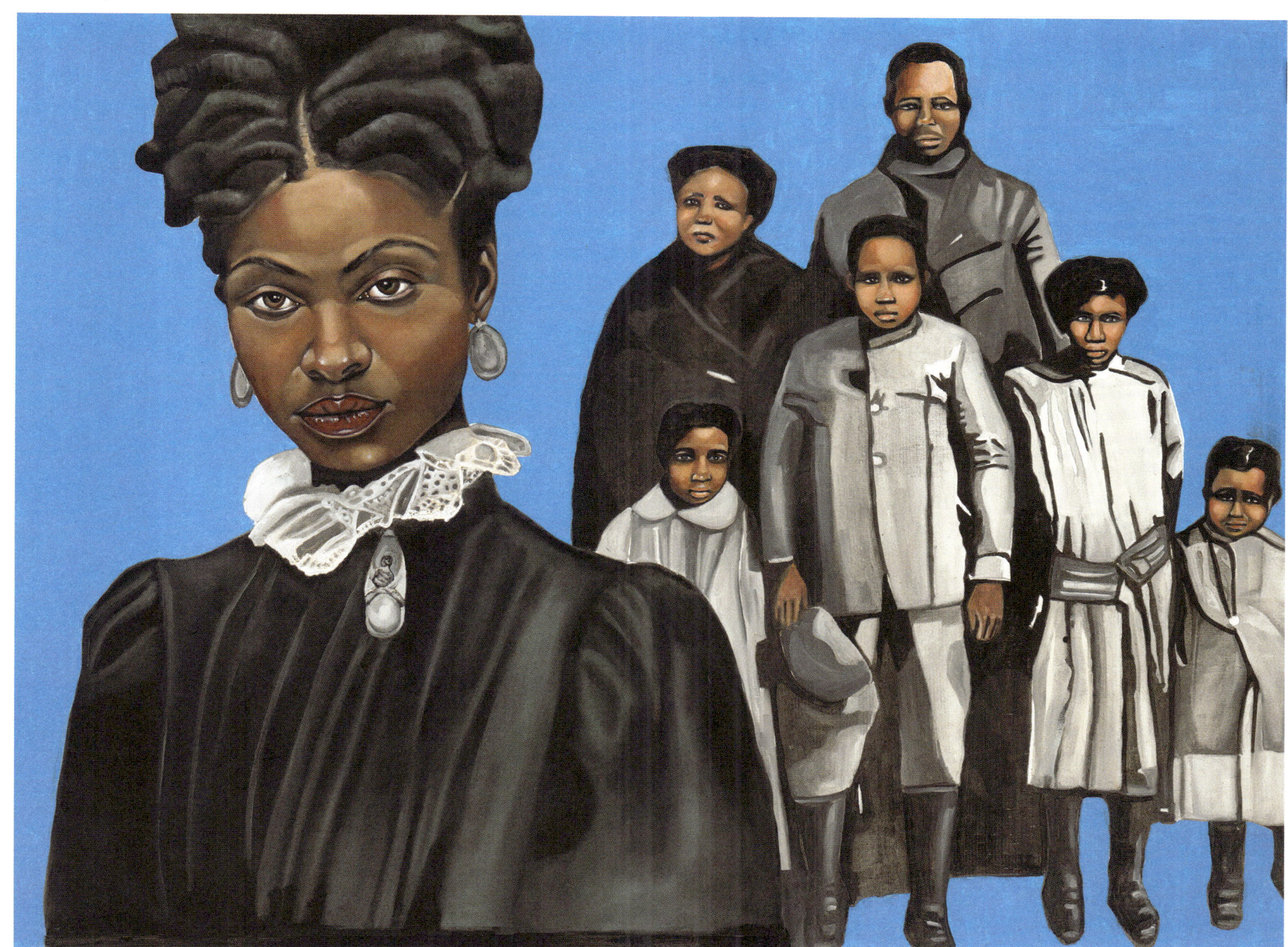

MY NAME IS

Harriett Walden. I was born in Jacksonville, Florida, raised in segregation in Sanford, Florida, in an all-Black township called Goldsboro.

I came to Seattle with my former husband from Santa Barbara, California, in 1975, to open a photography studio. He came here first, and then I followed with our four children, on the Greyhound bus. We got here, January 5th, 1975, and as the Greyhound bus was turning that corner on, on I-5, my second-oldest son, Chukundi Salisbury, said, "Mama, mama, mama, they've got the lights on in the city to welcome us," and all the people on the Greyhound bus clapped.

We moved into a motel out there on Aurora. I caught the bus downtown with all my children, because I didn't know anybody. In Woolworth's, one of my children was coughing. And this lady says, "Oh, what are you doing out here with that baby?" And I said, "Well, I just moved to Seattle, and we don't have a place to stay yet." And she says, "Oh, there's a place next door to me." She was just an African American lady who was nosy and that's a good characteristic sometimes.

It was a house that was owned by Dr. Harris, a dentist, down on 30th Avenue, and we moved into a basement apartment. Since he recognized that we still had our furniture in storage, he gave us two months' rent free, so we didn't have to pay any rent and could get our furniture out of storage.

We did open our photography studio. First, we were called Salisbury Beaver Photography. Mr. Beaver, who owned The Facts, gave us the money to open up our studio. And the next year, as the good man Mr. Beaver was, he came back and said, "Take my name off of the business, and just let it be Salisbury Photography. You have too many children to ever worry about paying me back." He gave us our start in Seattle.

MY NAME IS

John Yasutake. My parents are both Japanese Americans, born in the United States. I was born and raised in Chicago, specifically the area of Chicago's southside called Cottage Grove. On our floor we shared a common bathroom with two roommates who my mom and dad got to know from "camp." We call it "camp" but that was the internment camps during World War II.

My dad's from Washington state but was interned at Tule Lake, which was one of the high risk camps, the camp where they put folks they considered to be most un-American. My grandfather on my father's side had been, I guess you could say, a liaison to the Japanese government, for some of the logging camps. He had a special letter of dispensation from the emperor and he never renounced his Japanese citizenship, so he was considered high risk, most unpatriotic, a security issue. That's why the family all ended up at Tule Lake.

So we came here, from Chicago, to the Central Area, and that's where I grew up. My dad wasn't sufficiently situated to buy a home at that time, and my mom didn't work, so we shared a duplex with my dad's sister, Auntie Tomo. Dad had five sisters. He was the only male in the family, so he was treated like royalty. First born son, and the only son, in the traditional Japanese family, and my grandfather was seriously traditional. They dote on the first born son. They couldn't even feed him cold rice. They had to make a fresh pot of rice for lunch for him every day.

I started working before I was a teenager. Every summer. Worked on my uncle's brother's farm, and I mean hard work. We weren't picking fruit. We were digging, we were putting irrigation pipes down, we were driving tractors and trucks at eleven, twelve years old.

We lived on 25th Avenue South, between King and Lane street. That's pretty much as far north as we went. In our neighborhood there were several Japanese families. I remember Clifford Takuda, he became a state legislator, we used to call him Kippy, but his name was Clifford. His dad was George Takuda who had a drugstore in the Central District. But most families were African American, so the majority of the kids that I went to school with were African American. There were also quite a few Filipinos and then you had Native Americans too. I grew up with several families, the Shotwells, the DuPree family. We were all living in the Central Area. That's pretty much where we had to live.

ERIN SHIGAKI
Yasutake

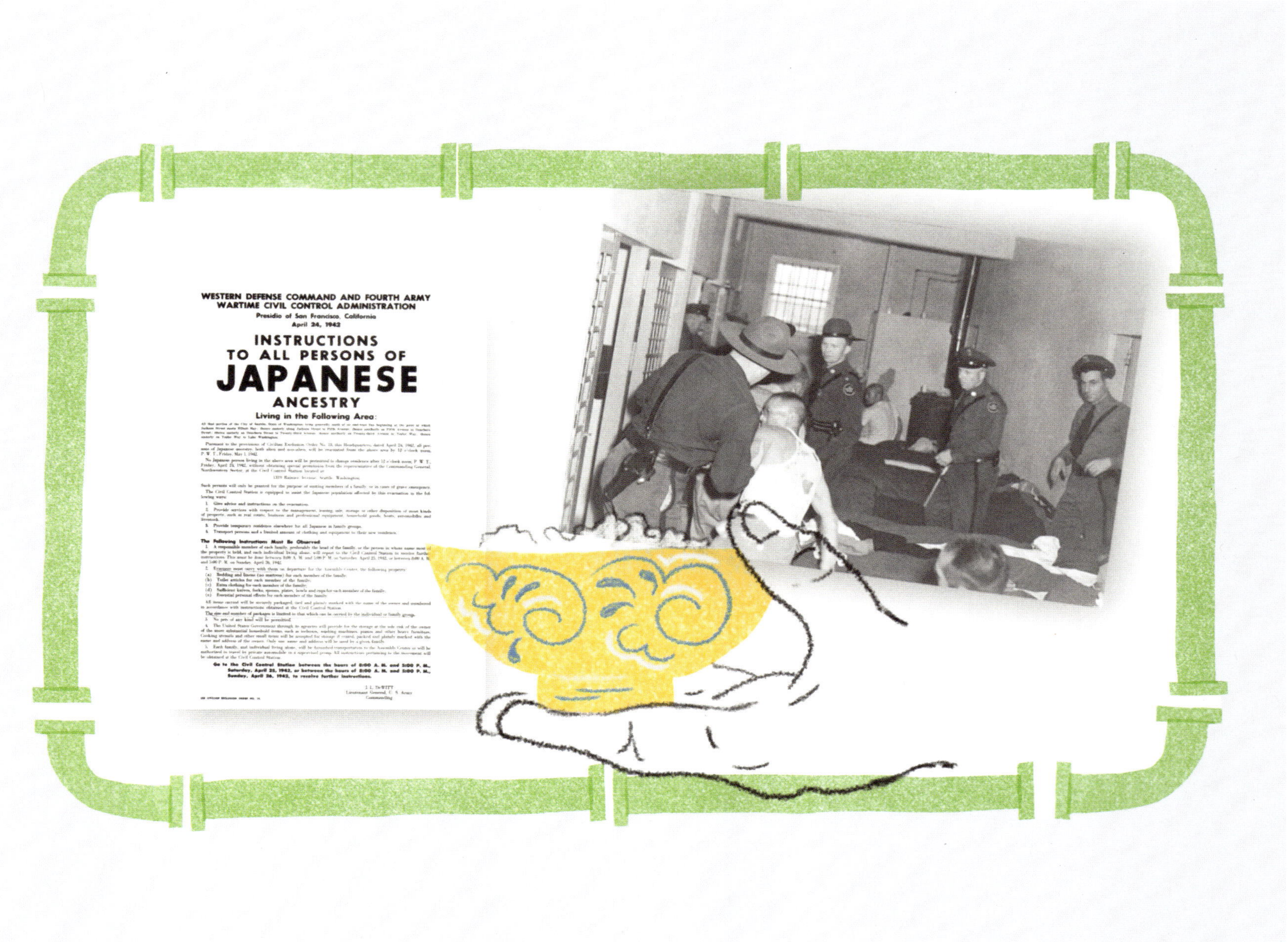

WESTERN DEFENSE COMMAND AND FOURTH ARMY
WARTIME CIVIL CONTROL ADMINISTRATION
Presidio of San Francisco, California
April 24, 1942

INSTRUCTIONS
TO ALL PERSONS OF
JAPANESE
ANCESTRY
Living in the Following Area:

The Following Instructions Must Be Observed

Go to the Civil Control Station between the hours of 8:00 A. M. and 5:00 P. M., Saturday, April 25, 1942, or between the hours of 8:00 A. M. and 5:00 P. M., Sunday, April 26, 1942, to receive further instructions.

J. L. DeWITT
Lieutenant General, U. S. Army
Commanding

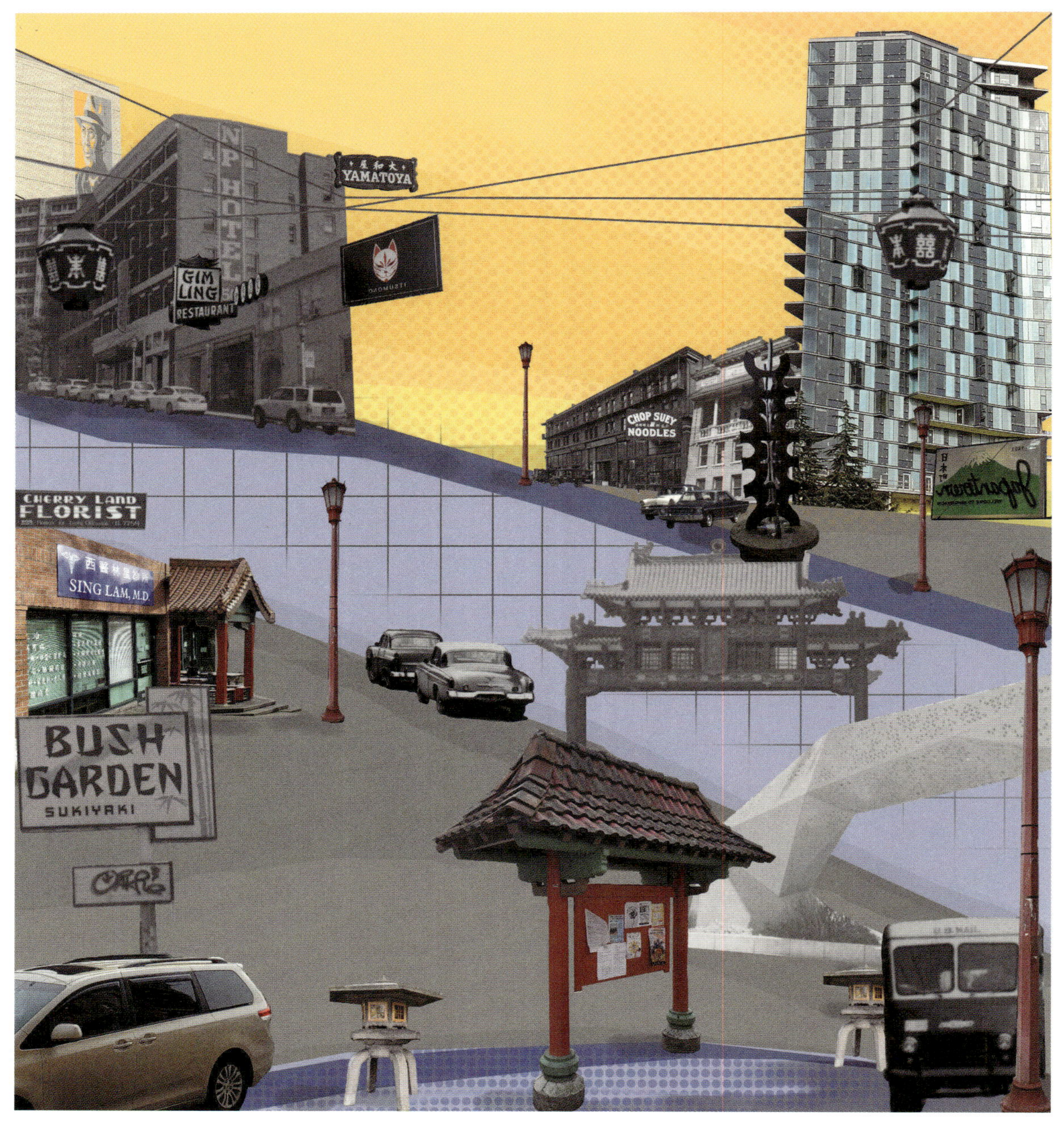

CHI MOSCOU-JACKSON
Untitled

WHEN WE GOT OFF THE PLANE

at SeaTac, we got a cab and my mother told the driver that she wanted to be in the Asian part of town. So the first place he took us was the Bush Hotel. My mother is in her tweed suit with her alligator purse, alligator pumps, and gloves, and she's walking to the door, and she sees all those men hanging around, so she comes back and tells him, "This—no good," So he pulled up to another hotel. It was very clean but old. The sign on the hotel said "NP Hotel" and we stayed there. I was twelve. I thought NP stood for "Negro People" *(laughs)*. I came to find out it stood for "Northern Pacific" *(laughs)*.

My mother got a job working in a sewing factory because she never worked before but she was an excellent seamstress. It was down on Rainier. Far West Garments. My father had been working as a stevedore in the army, but he couldn't get that job here. That was only for white people, in the 1960s. The unions didn't take Black people, so he ended up as a warehouseman.

My folks bought a house on 32nd and Dose Terrace. I made them buy that house because I wanted to go to a school that had some Black people. So it was either Garfield or Franklin, and this house was five blocks from Franklin, so I was happy about that! Our block was easily fifty percent Black. I think it was the Blackest block on Mount Baker. But, the next block over, there were no Black people. I had Asian friends too, but the thing was, we didn't go to each other's house, okay? The Asians didn't come to my house, I didn't go to their house, white kids didn't come to my house, and I didn't go to their house.

I was so happy for my mom that she could be in an area where there were other Asian people. She had Japanese friends; they were all war brides. The funny thing is the only war brides she had friendships with were women who were also married to Black soldiers. War brides who were married to white soldiers did not socialize with us at all.

Annie Harper

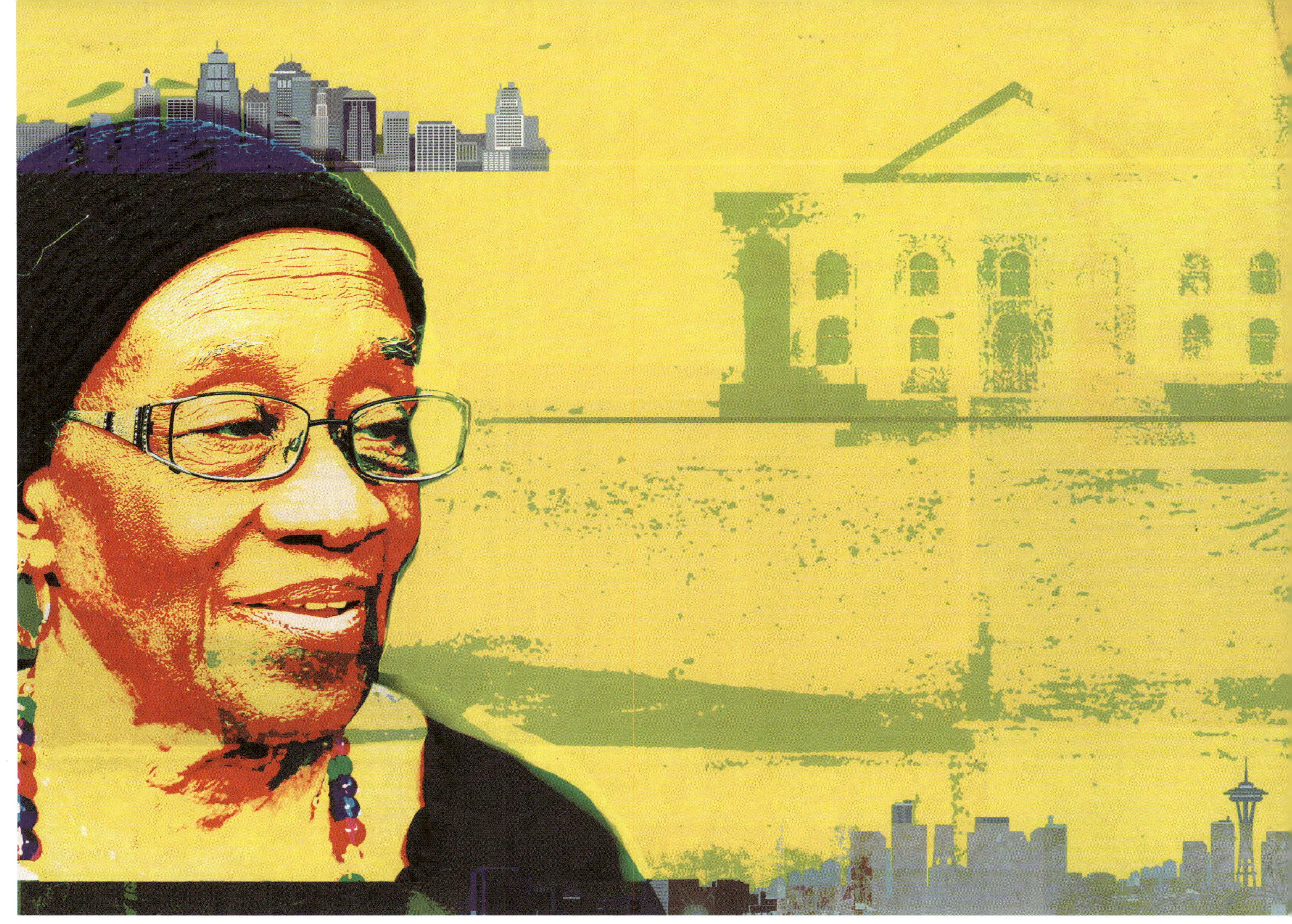

MY NAME IS

Alice Yvonne Lory Thomas. I was born in Kansas City, in 1931. It was General Hospital Number Two, which was for Black patients. Number One was for white patients.

When my mother was pregnant with the next child, she asked my uncle and his wife Lydia if they could keep me until my mother was better. Seventeen years later was how long I lived with them. Some people say, "Oh that was not good." It was good for me because, at my uncle's house, I was treated like an only child.

We were not rich people. My uncle was a hard-working man, a janitor. I remember every Friday night he would bring home the Kansas City Call, which was a Black newspaper in Kansas City. We would sit down and he would read. He had a third grade education, but he knew how to read, so we would have that and we would have a Pepsi. That was our Friday night ritual.

So, I had a very full life until March 1948, when my aunt passed away. My parents said that I was to come and live with them. I think my mother realized that I was a very sad little girl. So she wrote to her sister who lived out here, in Seattle, and asked could I come out here and go to college. They arranged it, and I got myself on the train and came out to Seattle.

Within a month of arriving, I joined Mount Zion. I didn't do any checking around. I didn't try to see what other people were doing. I simply joined. Now, I was a pew warmer, but I was a faithful one.

JITE AGBRO
Alice Thomas

I came from segregation.

But my aunt told me, when I got here, "You can go sit anywhere you want."

People can tell you something, but you have to experience it yourself.

I remember there was a little restaurant on 3rd and Union, across from the post office. I stood and looked, and stood and looked, and thought, "I'm not sure I'm gonna go in there." But finally, I got myself together and just opened the door and went in and sat down.

Not long after I arrived, I started at the University of Washington. We had a little group of Black people. We sat at the table together and had our lunch, and I remember the guy who was over at the Urban League tried to tell us to spread out. But we weren't gonna spread out. We didn't have anybody to spread out to! I got my bachelors, and my masters, in sociology and social work and eventually

I became the Director of Family Court at the Superior Court of King County, and stayed there 17 years.

I remember that one of the attorneys said to me, "You know, the judge is really brave."

And I thought, "Brave about what?"

He said, "That he hired you." It was brave that the white judge hired me.

Another time, a guy was out at the front desk and asked to see the director.

I came trotting to the front of the office, and he was shocked.

He said, "I wanna see the director."

I said, "I am the director."

MY NAME IS

Vicky Ann Bernadette Garner. I was born in San Antonio, Texas, and moved to Seattle with my mother and my maternal grandparents, when I was nine years old. My grandfather had two sisters that were living here and were desperately trying to get him to move here. He was kind of an entrepreneur. He owned a record shop, he owned a jukebox business, and he was also a contractor, a carpenter, but he could never join the unions. He didn't look Black, because he was half white, but he would never...on applications he always put that he was, at that time, "negro," and carpentry unions did not accept Blacks then.

He started working at Foss Tug and Launch. My mom got a job with the Central Area Motivation Program, and from there, she went to the Model Cities Program. She was a housing relocation specialist.

I was at 913 20th Avenue for the majority of my life. My family owned that house. They could not look for a house in any other neighborhood than the Central District. When we moved in, the neighborhood was Black and white. It didn't happen until the latter part of the '60s that the whites moved out.

MY NAME IS

Al Doggett. I was born in Brooklyn, New York. And I came out to Seattle, in 1967.

I'm a commercial artist, and I had been working with art studios in New York, one pretty major studio, which was sort of the dream studio, and that was really great, because I got to do the kind of creative work that I wanted to do. But, after a while, I got a little bored with New York. I wanted something different. I grew up there, and I was curious about what was going on on the West Coast.

My mother had told me that her sister lived in a place called Tacoma, Washington. I took the map out, and it was funny because I really wanted to get as far away from New York as possible. I looked at the map, and Washington was way up in this corner. So, I took the train out, three day trip. I got to Tacoma, and it was just sky, water, mountains. I said "Man, I would love to live out here."

I did go back to New York, and I worked more and learned more there. But eventually I went to the New York Public Library and got a Seattle phone book, and I looked up advertising agencies and sent letters. I got five replies. They said "Yeah, we need people. Come on out."

So, that was it. We saved and came back out here in 1967. We stayed in a

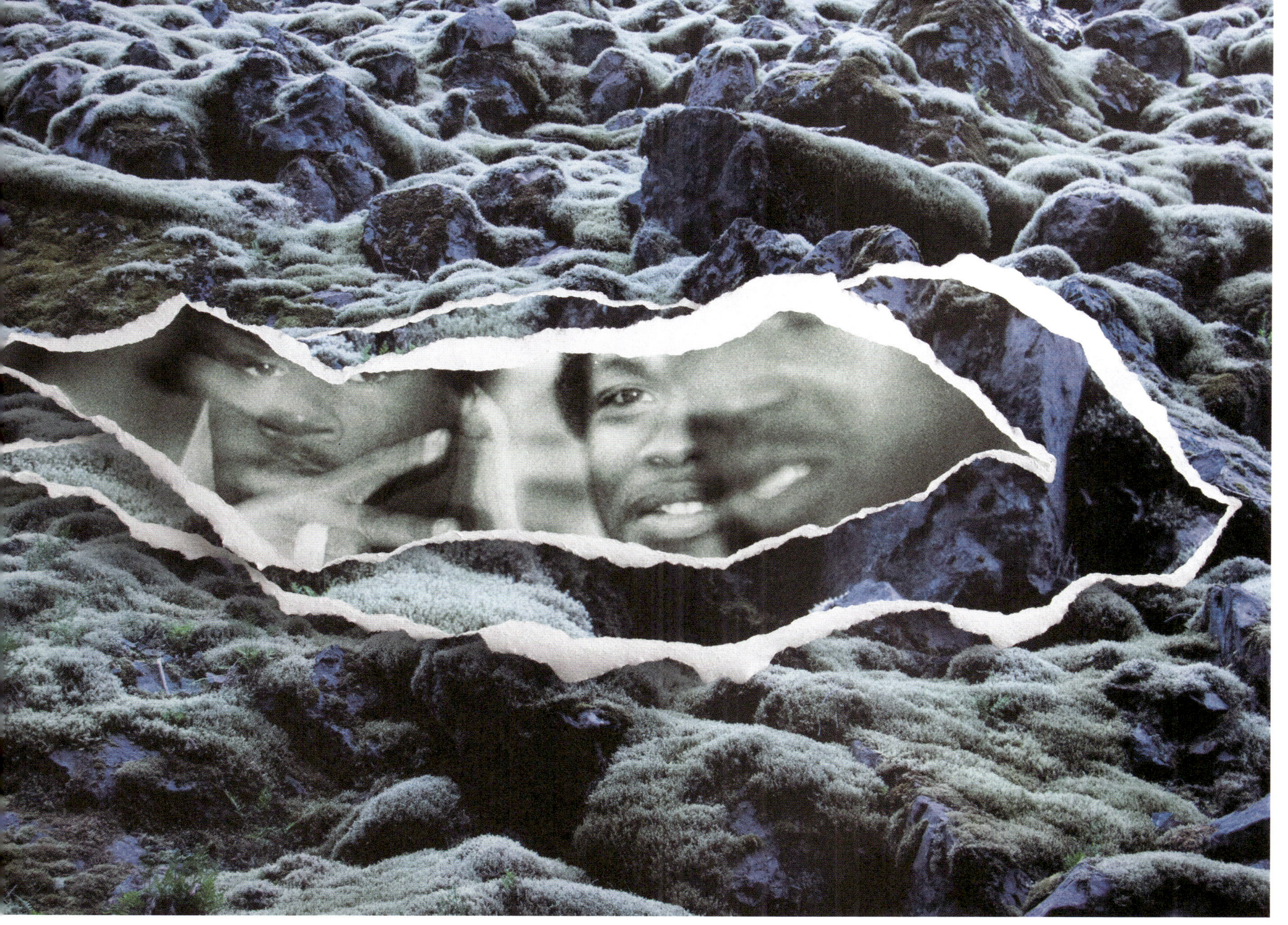

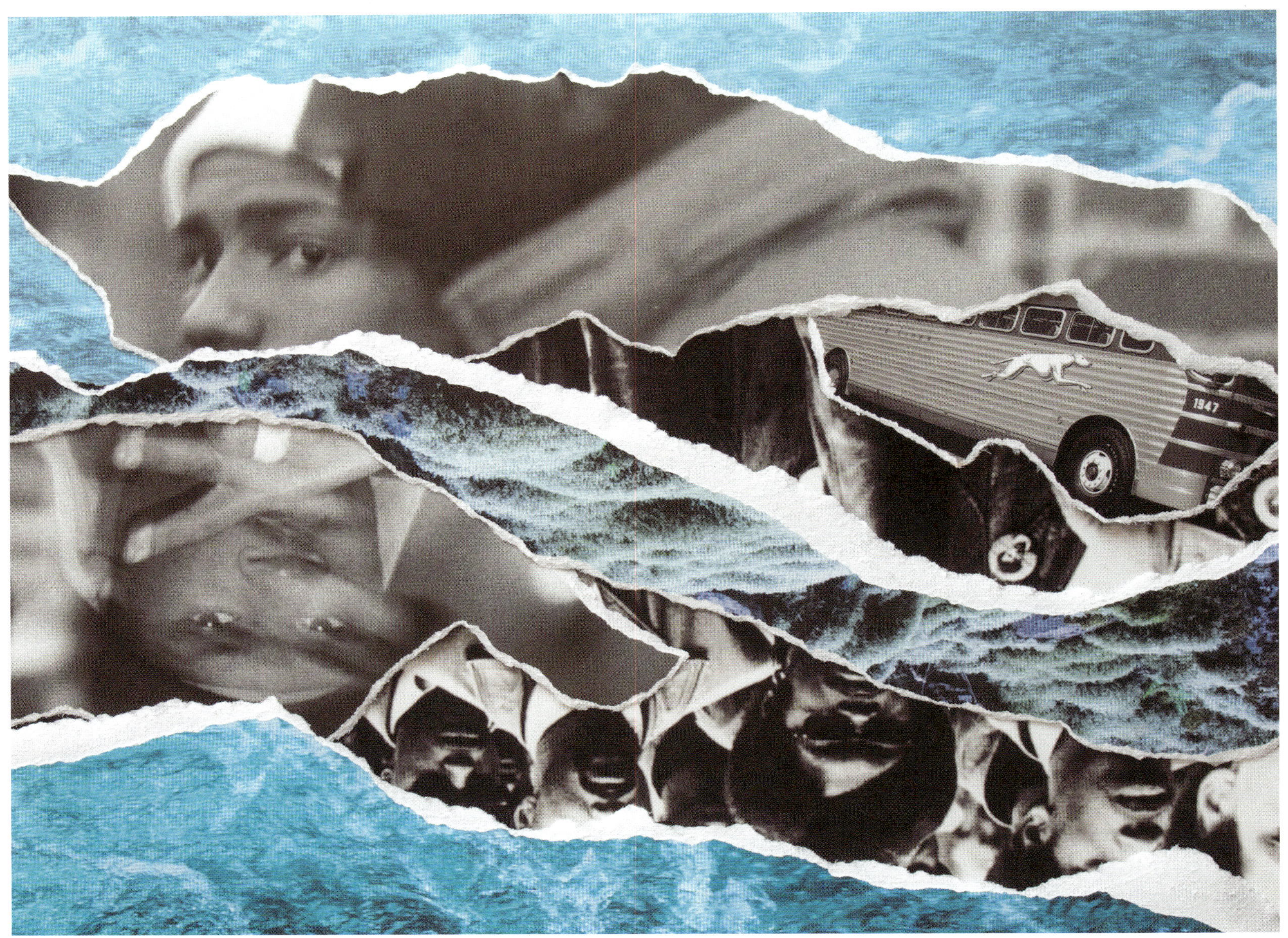

1947

hotel downtown for a few days. We saw some Black folks downtown getting on the bus, so, "Hey, wonder where they're going. Let's follow." The bus came into the Central District, and we just started walking. There was a real estate office on the corner of 34th and Union. We went in there and asked about apartments, cause that's how people lived in New York.

The gentleman said, "Did you ever think of renting a house?"

We said "House? A whole house?" That's what people did here. He showed us this house. It was raw. It was 103 dollars a month. We moved in.

I had the five letters from the agencies, so I went to the first contact, saw the receptionist, and told her who I was here to see.

She did a double take.

I waited.

The art director came out, and I had talked to him on the phone, so he knew I was coming.

Another double take.

They didn't know I was Black. But they saw my portfolio and loved it and a couple of days later I got a call. It slowly built from there.

But it took a while to get to know the people in our neighborhood. It was kind of strange. People didn't reach out that quickly, that easily. This area right here was, except for the next door neighbor, all white. I got the sense that the white families were moving out, almost like they needed to get out because there were Blacks moving in. This was 1967, '68. The Black Panthers had their headquarters down the street on Union. But, you know, if you didn't go to Garfield, no one knew you.

But there was a basketball court down the street. I used to go down and play basketball with the kids, the Black kids in the community. They're the first people I met, the kids playing basketball.

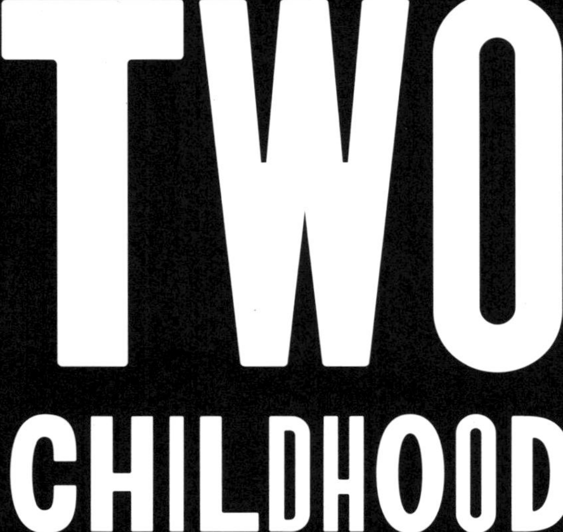

TWO
CHILDHOOD

Growing up in the Central Area was the single
greatest experience of my life. It taught me
most everything in terms of my values and how
I relate to people, and how to serve and engage
people. I wouldn't trade that experience for
anything in the world. It was a self-contained
neighborhood. You stayed in your neighborhood,
and everything you needed was in that
neighborhood.

John Yasutake

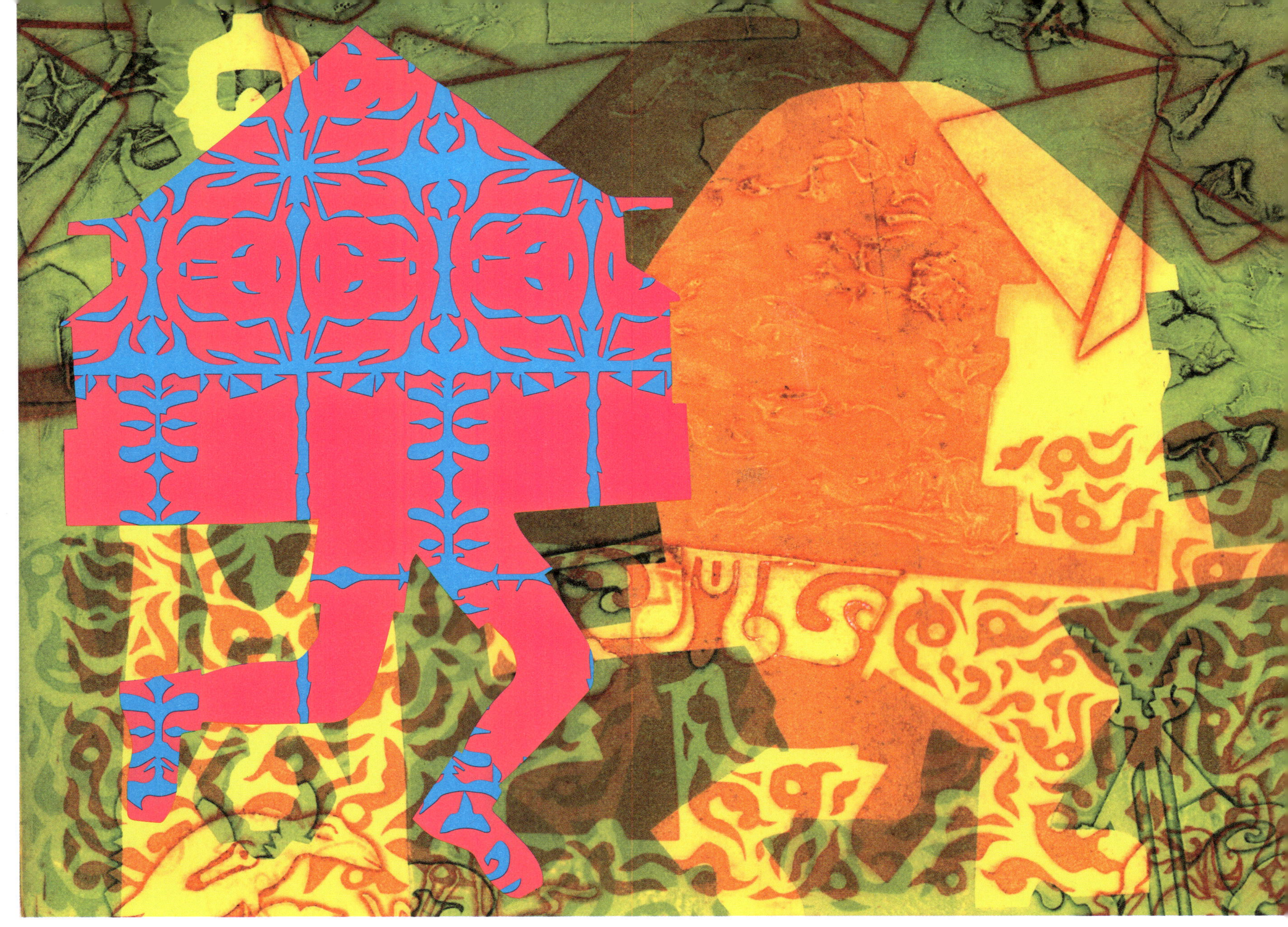

MY NAME IS

Marie Kidhe. I was born in Seattle, Washington. My parents are Ugandan immigrants, and I'm their first American-born child. I lived in the Central District all my life.

When my parents first came to Seattle, in the early 70s, they were told to move to the Central District, because that's where all the Black people live. It was good and it was not so good. It was good because, at that stage in my parents' marriage, and in their learning how to be here, all the Africans that we knew lived in the CD. Our relatives that had already come were close by, like my uncle Ben Abe, who still runs the travel agency up in Madrona.

But there weren't a lot of Africans. That whole migration didn't really start until the '90s. So there were times when people didn't know how to take us. We're of a nice, darker complexion so sometimes people were really rattled by that, and my parents had some issues. My father got into some fights with other Black men over bad things said, and my mom, sometimes we would be in places and get a lot of stares. But I still feel like this was the best place for my parents to be.

Back then the CD was just a lot different.

It felt like there was always somewhere to go.

It felt limitless.

At that time, your neighbors were the kids you went to school with, so all you needed was a bike and some energy and you were gone. We'd walk downtown. That was nothing. There'd be like twenty

ROMSON BUSTILLO
Marie Kidhe

of us walking downtown. It just seemed easy. There was always someone's house you could stop at, or there was always somebody who knew you and could holler out their window to tell you to go home or whatever.

I loved, loved, loved, loved, loved the Black Festival. I looked forward to it every year. We would always watch it in front of Roger's Thriftway, on Union and Martin Luther King, but back then it was Empire Way. I felt like that was just something magical in the CD. All the kids you went to school with, and their families, on the corner with tents and chairs and blankets. I was always too scared to be in the parade. I wanted to be in the drill team so bad, but I was really shy back then.

I spent many, many Saturdays at DeCharlene's on Madison. It was hot. Because she didn't have no AC, and it was pressing irons, and dryers, and roller sets. My brother hated it. He had

to come. It was an all-day process. My mom would pack two lunches for us because it would be my mom getting her hair done, and then me getting my hair done. We always went on a Saturday, and it would literally be an all-day function, but I loved it, because I've always been into hair and fashion. She would have these extraordinary dresses from all these different places, boutique glamor dresses, and, if I was good, sometimes, I'd get a dress. And then she just had this plethora of hats. She has always been a beautiful blond, so you'd come in to see what blond look she was rocking this weekend. She would always be selling tickets for some community event that was going on. So sometimes she'd have to stop 'cause she'd need to go to the front desk and sell a ticket for Ebony Fair or something. I loved it. It was my opportunity to see beauty.

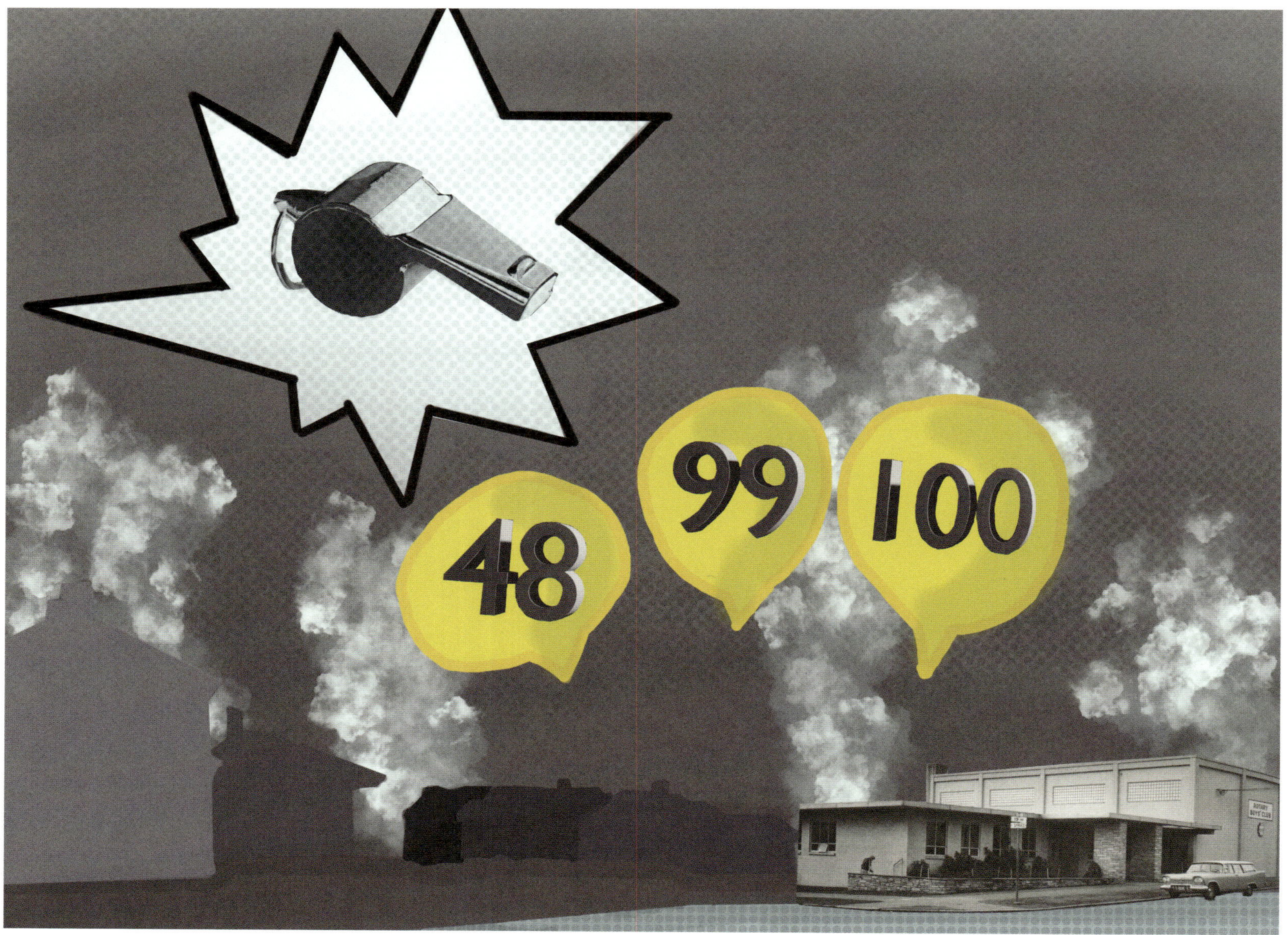
48
99
100

THE BOYS CLUB

was a second home for me. That's where everybody would congregate. We played baseball, football, basketball at the Boys Club. They had arts and crafts in one section. They had a piano room. A library.

My mom would know exactly where we were. We weren't allowed to go anywhere else. We did, of course. But that's where we hung out, at the Boys Club.

Everybody in the community went there. Chinese, Japanese, and the Jewish kids. And you had a card with your name on it and we were divided into groups by age. At 8:30 in the evening they got on the microphone, "Time for all Midgets and Juniors to go home." The Boys Club would stay open an extra thirty minutes for the older kids.

Of all the directors of the Boys Club, I remember Mr. Gully. Black gentleman. Six foot two. Ex-army sergeant. And, he did not play. He did not play.

One of the things he would make us do was push ups. One time, we were smoking outside, behind the Boys Club. I was too chicken to inhale, so, I'm puffing away. Somebody must have smelled it or told Mr. Gully. I take a little puff, and as I walk out into the open, there's Mr. Gully standing in the stairway and the smoke comes out of my mouth.

Gully says, "Lockhart!!! Who else is with you?!"
"Robert Shine."

"Shine! Are you smoking!?"

"No, mmm mmm".

"Give me a hundred push ups."

He's yelling so loud, half the Boys Club is there. One big tall kid with a basketball is looking at us and laughing so Gully says to him, "Johnson, you watch Lockhart and make sure he does them push ups!"

This big kid did not want to be there to watch this little skinny, bony kid do one hundred push ups. So he's counting like, "one, two, twenty-five, forty-eight, ninety-nine, one hundred."

I did three push ups.

"Lockhart, you do your push ups? Did he do his push ups?"

"Yes, Mr. Gully."

Never forget that. The Boys Club was a catalyst for a lot of kids growing up in that area, in the right direction. The community felt like a watched over community.

Daryl Lockhart

A LOT OF LOCAL BUSINESSES,

a number of restaurants, barber shops, a record store, a drug store. Right down the street, Mr Preston would cut hair. There was a furniture store, the shoe shine man, later on there was Scotty's Pool Hall. All owned by local families, African American, Asian, and Jewish. Basically, people who lived in the neighborhood and worked in the neighborhood. If it weren't for the fact that I grew up in this neighborhood, in this community, I don't think I would be the person I am today.

John Yasutake

THE FIRST HOUSE

I remember was on 16th and Fir. The neighbors were a lot of immigrant families. Norwegians, Swedes, Jews, the Irish. A Jewish woman would always call us kids up to her house to give us spinach cakes. I hated spinach, but I loved those spinach cakes. And the adults in the neighborhood knew all the kids. Everybody played together, so everybody learned to know whose child belonged to who, and they'd look out for us and holler at us and, if they could catch us, swat us on the butt.

There wasn't very many locked doors.

Locked doors came later.

Mark Cook

MY FAMILY WAS

the first family on the block to have a color TV. This was like 1967, and we carried the TV in the house, and everybody on the block stood on the porch, and went like, "Ooh, color TV."

Bonanza in color. *The Fugitives* in color.

We had a Zenith, "the quality goes in before the name goes on." A floor-model with the AM/FM radio, the turntable, and the twenty-six-inch TV. My mother would say no watching TV while she was gone to work. That's when TVs had these big vac-uum tubes in the back. You had to turn the TV on and let it warm up before your program came on. So we would put a piece of plastic on top of the TV, a wet towel with ice, and watch TV, and then take it off when she came home, because the first thing my mom did when she came home was put her hand on top of the TV to see if it was warm, If you think about it, if that water would have dripped in the back of that TV and hit one of those picture tubes, the party would have been over.

Gregory Scott

WE KNEW EVERYBODY

blocks around. All the kids came to our house because our house sat on a double lot. We'd all gather there. My mother and father paid for so many broken windows in the neighbor's house. I don't know why but, if we played kickball or baseball or something, the ball always went through their windows. We ran through everybody's yards. We had peach trees, cherry trees, blackberries. Neighbors had raspberries, apples, all kinds of fruit. Nobody yelled or screamed at you to get out of their yard or anything like that.

I mean, there were more children in the neighborhood that called our mother "Mother" than anybody else. We didn't refer to anybody else's mother as "Mother" or "Mommy." But they referred to my mother as "Mother."

Narvella Jackson

PHOTO BY
JILL FREIDBERG

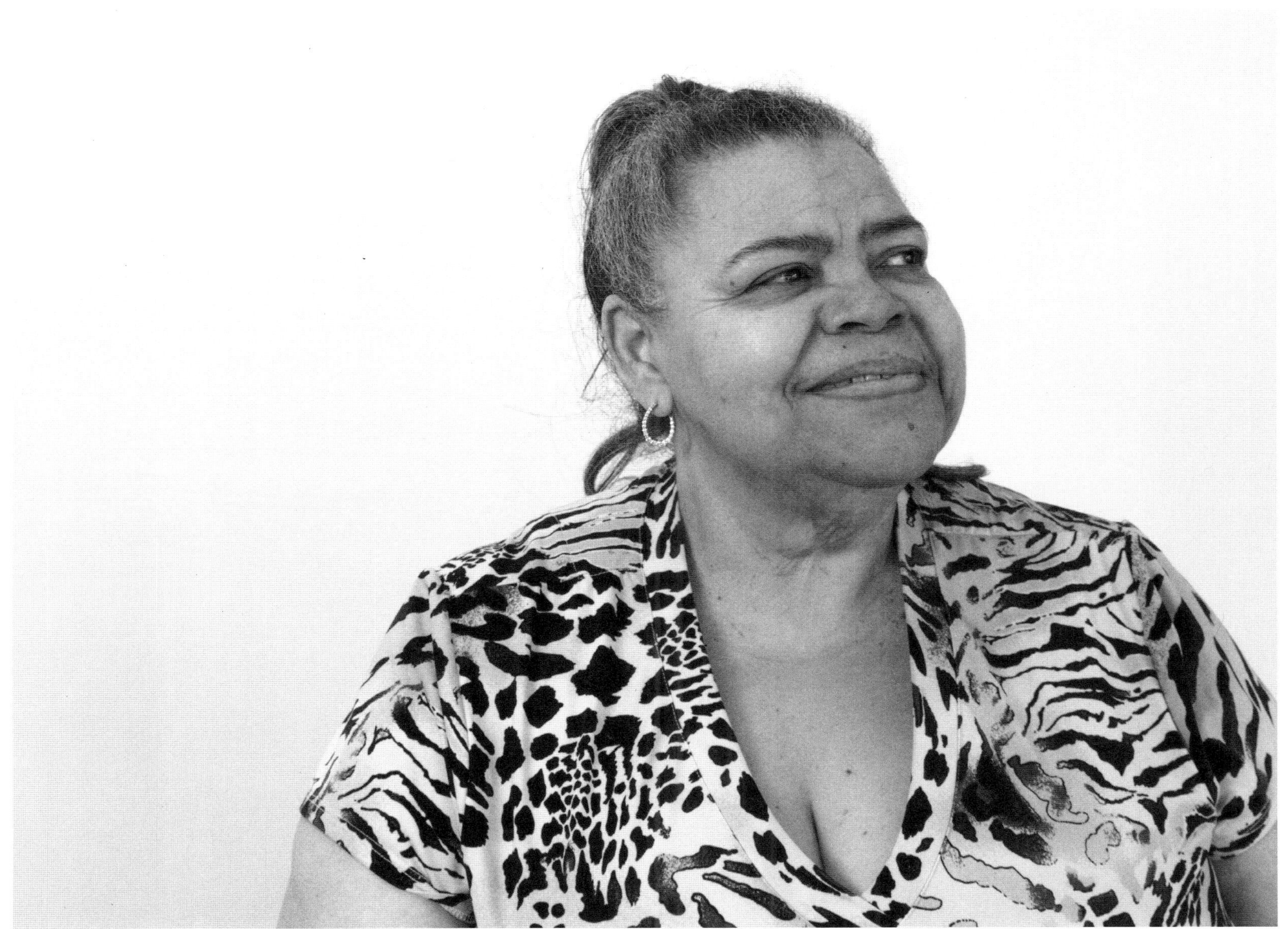

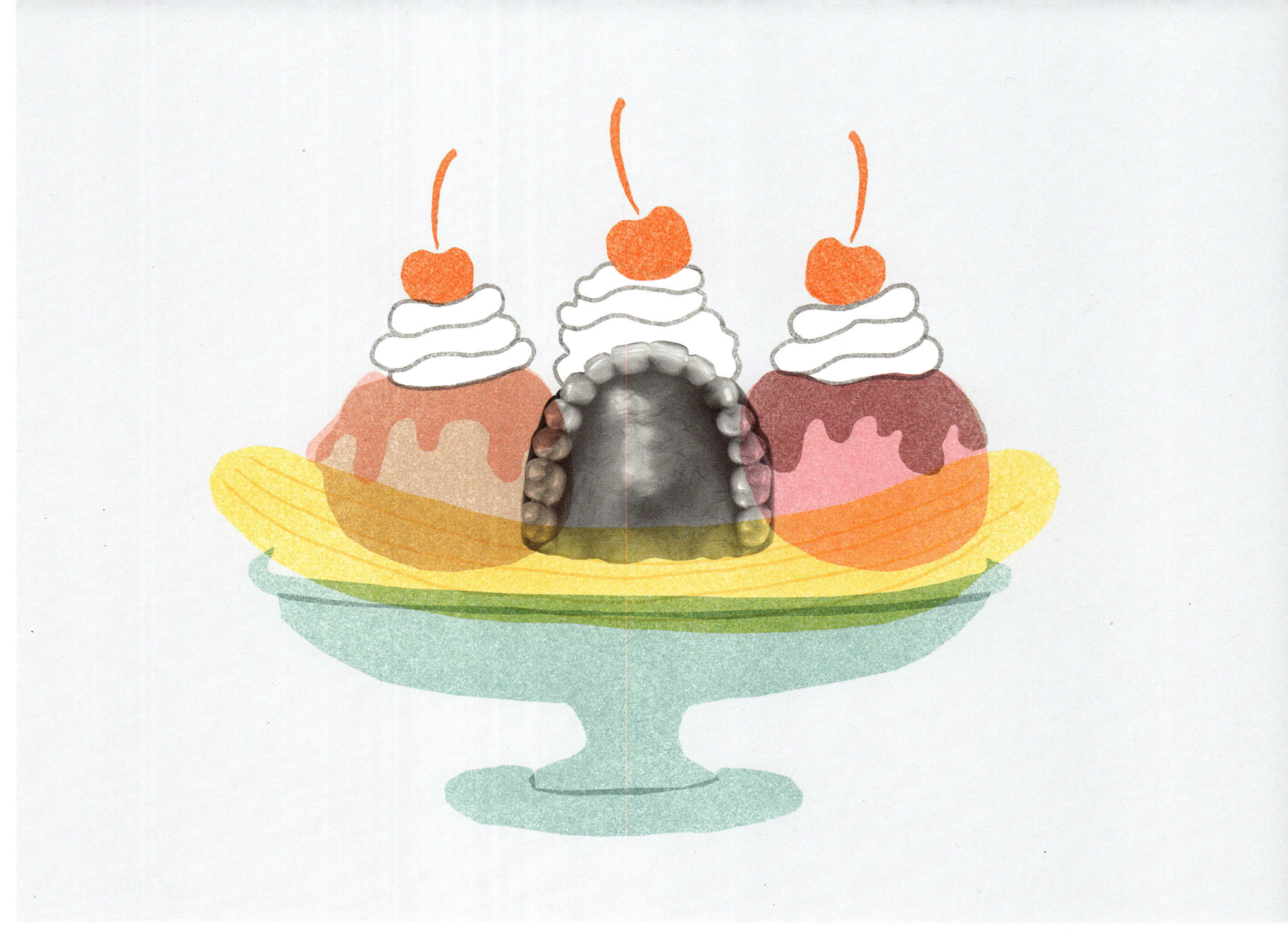

THE CENTRAL AREA

was like an extended village, and it was very
multicultural. I mean next door to us, when we
moved in, the family was Japanese, and Jewish
families lived all around us.There was a white
lady, I can't remember her name. On Halloween
she would leave the door unlocked and have
bowls of candy sitting out on the counter and
we were on our honor just to come in and get
the candy and be polite about it. We had a few
knuckleheads who wanted to just grab the whole
bowl, but we didn't allow it.

We knew everybody, and everybody knew us,
and everybody knew my parents. We had a party
line when we first moved in. My mother got rid
of that quick.

Everything was there. The stores. The doc-
tor's office. Dr Robert Joyner was on Madison.
We had the Madrona movie theater and the Roy
Cross movie theater. You didn't go downtown.
Only fast, misbehaved children went downtown.
You went to your neighborhood movie theater.
I mean there were Black cleaners, Black restau-
rants, Black hair shops, record stores. We had
Mr Gideon's drugstore and pharmacy. He had
a big soda fountain shop where he made the
best banana splits in the whole world. I got one
free once.

I was waiting for my auntie, who worked for
Dr. Joyner, and I went down to the drugstore
with just enough for a six cent soda, but I really
wanted a banana split. I walked in the door.
Mr. Gideon said to me, "I'll give you whatever
you want if you just don't tell anybody what
you saw."

I looked around, and I didn't see anything
unusual.

I wanted that banana split.

I said, "sure!" I hopped up on the stool, and I
kept looking trying to figure out what it is I'm
not supposed to tell, cause I don't wanna tell,
and what if he grills me about it, what if he asks
me.

I got the banana split and it was great. He
said, "If you tell anybody you saw me without
my teeth."

I hadn't noticed! I didn't know teeth came out.
He could have gone the whole day and never
said a word to me and I never would have
noticed. I figure that since he's passed away for
about twenty years now, I can tell.

Phyllis Beatty Yasutake

I GREW UP WITH

a Japanese guy. We lived across the street from each other. My mother, Black woman from Oklahoma, made sukiyaki because Kenny's mom taught her how to make it. My childhood friends were Asian, Jews, Black folks. And there were some white folks, too.

You walked everywhere. There was no fear to walk around the neighborhood. We could walk down to the lake and pick blackberries. We walked to Garfield for track practice. I would walk to all my baseball games. I walked to the arboretum. I had to walk everywhere because we had one car. My dad drove that car to work. And my mom didn't drive. That was the thing. She didn't drive. My dad said, "My wife is not going to work." I mean, he was adamant about it.

There was a Jewish woman across the street who taught piano to all the kids in the neighborhood. The next-door neighbor, an older Jewish man, would always talk to the kids and say "shalom." He'd grab you by the face, you know, "shalom." We were all in the neighborhood together. Then the Jewish man next door moved out. Black family moved in. The piano teacher across the street moved out. A Black family moved in. By the '70s, I had seen that transition.

Steve Sneed

WHEN I WAS AROUND FIVE,

my parents signed me up for little league football at Judkins Park, from age five to thirteen, I played for the CD Panthers. Growing up, the CD wasn't the safest place and I know a lot of my aunties and my mom looked out for me and my friends. Any friends that I played football with, or went to school with, I knew their moms. Our moms knew each other. They would just make sure that we were safe. Anyone's mom was like your mom.

And the coaches! Coach T was my first-ever little league football coach and then Coach Chris. Those two were kind of like my other dads when I was at football practice, positive male role models, which when I was younger was hard to find. I just love every adult that's ever seen me grow up around this neighborhood.

Sky Sawyer

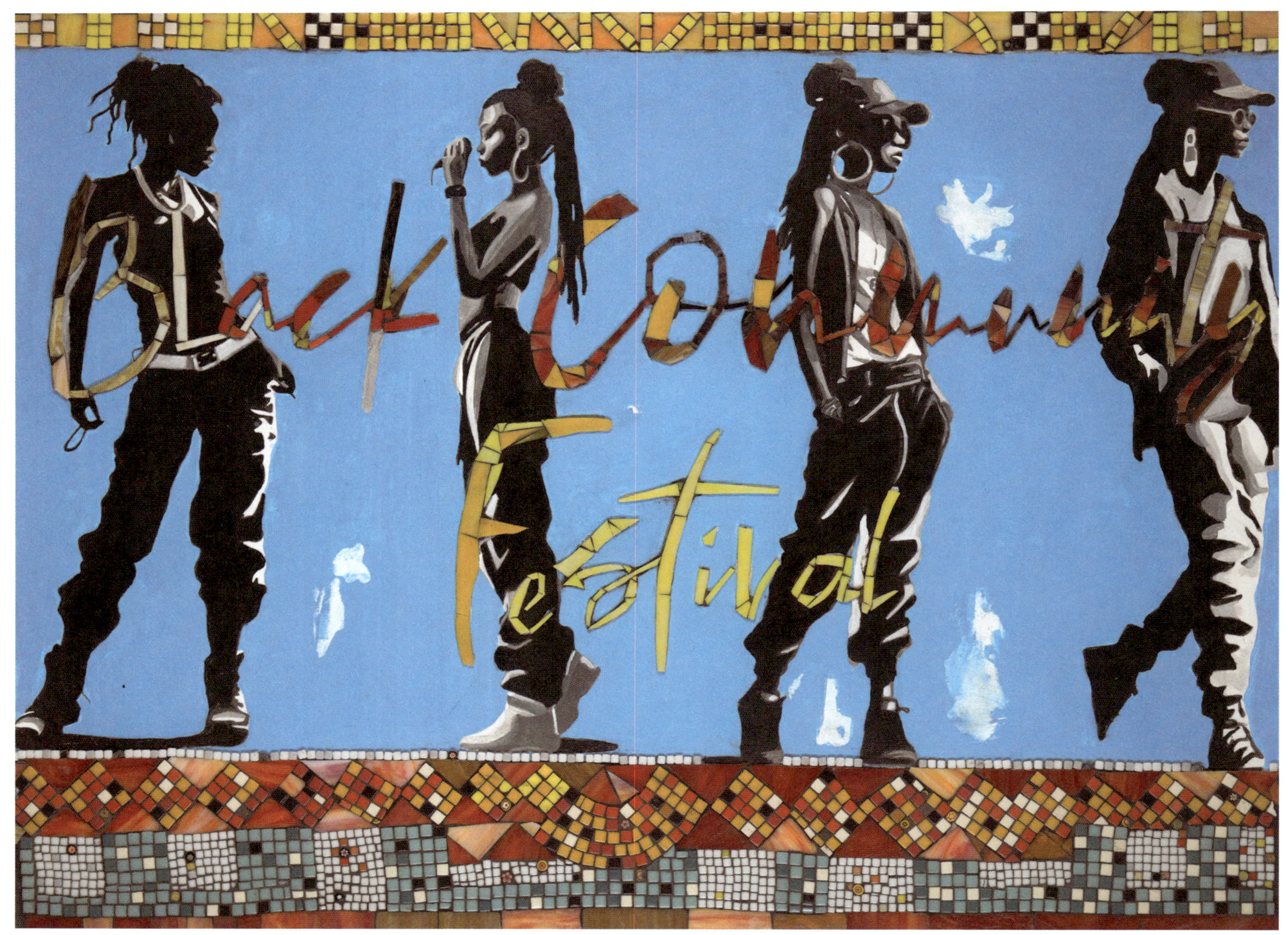

Black Community
Festival

MY NAME IS

BONNIE HOPPER
Untitled

Lulu Miles. I was born here in Seattle, and I was raised in the Central District, so I know it like the back of my hand. My parents bought the house that they live in five days before I was born and they've been in that house over forty years.

My dad is from Beggs, Oklahoma, and he grew up with fifteen or sixteen siblings on a farm. And then, around age eight, they came up here to Seattle for a better life. My mom was born in Monroe, Louisiana. Same story, raised down there, came up here with a foster mom after her mom passed. My mom and dad met when my mom and her two sisters were singers, in church. They went to the same church their whole lives, so they've known each other since they were eight.

My dad was a parole officer, and after that he joined Local 32, plumbers and pipefitters, for many, many years until he hurt his knee. My mom worked for King County Metro Transit; she was a rider telephone operator.

I went to St. Therese growing up, and then I begged my dad to let me go to a public school, but I needed to try a different school, before I went to Garfield 'cause I was, like, "Ooh it's too fresh for me." So I ended up going to Eckstein my eighth-grade year, and then I went to Garfield for four years and had a blast. I had a neighborhood crew. We would all hang out on the porch. We would play Double Dutch or we would take our bikes and just kind of get lost. I had so much freedom because I just felt a sense of family wherever I went, you know, you could go down the street, pleasant looks, comfortable.

The Black Community Festival that took place down on MLK, it was huge. I'm talking huge. I'm talking, you would walk down that street from Catfish Corner used to be all the way up to the park. Each step you would take you'd be like, "Oh my god, that's such-and-such." You couldn't see across the street, you know, it was just packed, hundreds of people, and I'm not being dramatic. It was just brown people everywhere, and it was just family.

MY NAME IS

Aretha Basu. I was born in Pennsylvania, and I grew up here in the CD, from the age of five. I grew up right between the Odessa Brown Clinic and SVI, in the apartments between Jackson and Yesler.

Most of the people who lived in my apartments were Latinx folks. I was the only Indian kid. It used to feel very cozy. We used to have parties in the streets and you'd wake up in the morning and hear all the uncles blasting banda music, and all the kids would be running around. We used to have barbecues every weekend in the park behind our apartment building. We'd hang piñatas from the very top floor of the apartment building, and all the rugrats would come and bust these piñatas open, and the whole block would be covered in candy litter.
It felt safe and comfortable. People wouldn't even lock their doors. All the moms would just leave their doors open. We would be running in and out. If you're hungry, just go to someone's house and get some food. All the moms used to feed all the kids.

My parents got divorced when I was young and my mom moved away, so I was just with my dad. It was really important to him that I knew how to speak Spanish. So he was always saying, "Go to your friends' houses, learn the culture, eat the food, speak Spanish, and do all of that." But the second I walked through our door, it was an Indian household. He was very strict. Some of the traditional values he had, he still tried to hold onto within our house. It was like two different worlds. The first dances I learned were cumbia and banda. That was the first music that I was introduced to. Then I would go home and my dad would be singing old Bengali songs.

My dad would try to cook, and he was not a good cook. For example, he would take the Swedish meatballs from Ikea and make a curry out of it that was very strange tasting. He would make dishes for all the different moms, because they took care of me, and none of the moms liked the food. And everyone was too embarrassed to tell him. So everyone had Tupperwares full of my dad's food and just didn't eat it.

My dad loved living here. He always felt very loved and accepted by the people that lived in the apartments around us. He said, "I may not understand a lot of the culture here, but I trust the people here. I know that if anything were to happen to me, they would step in and they'd take care of you." And they did. The day my dad died, all the residents were in my house, taking care of me.

PHOTO BY
JILL FREIDBERG

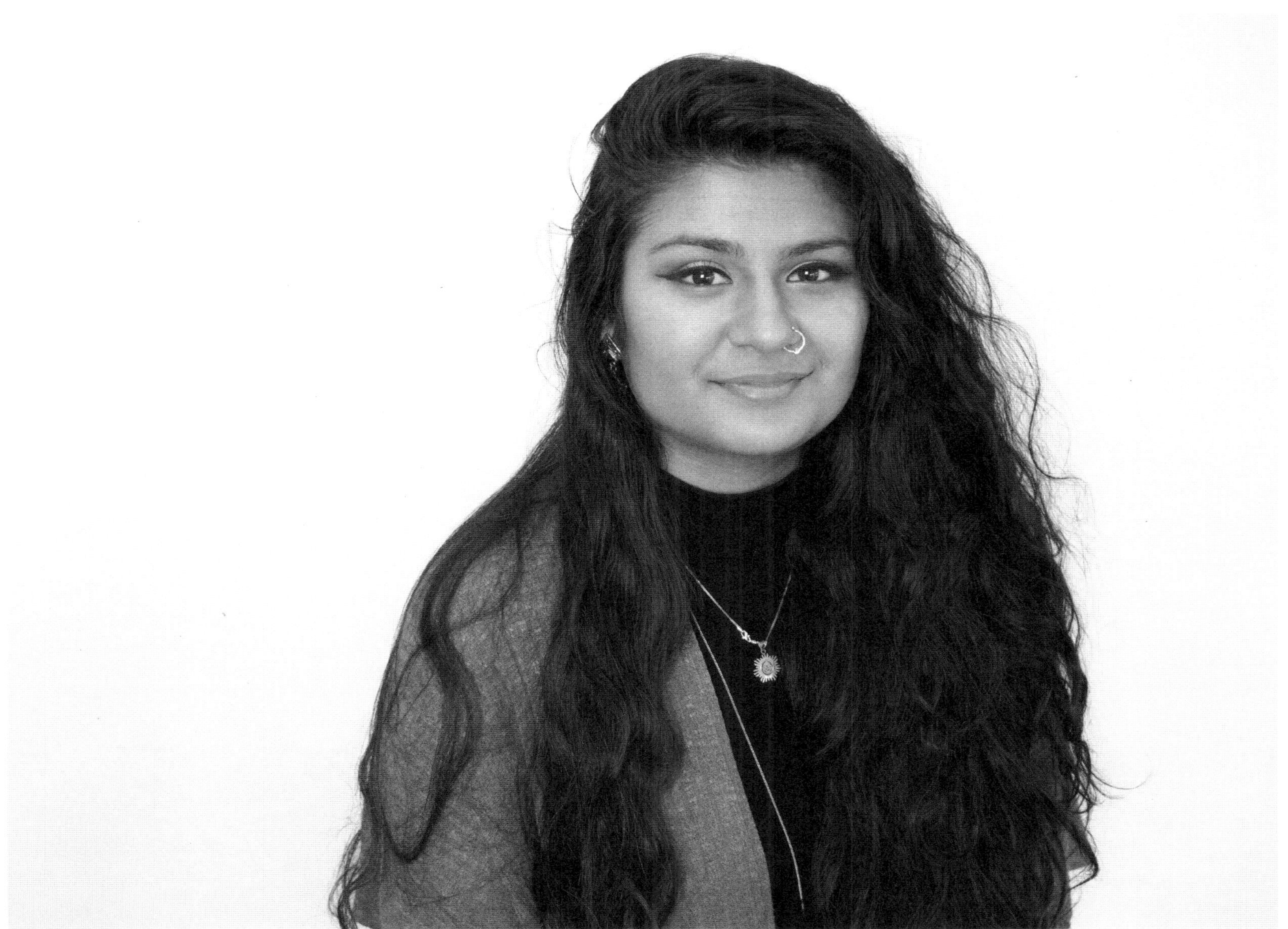

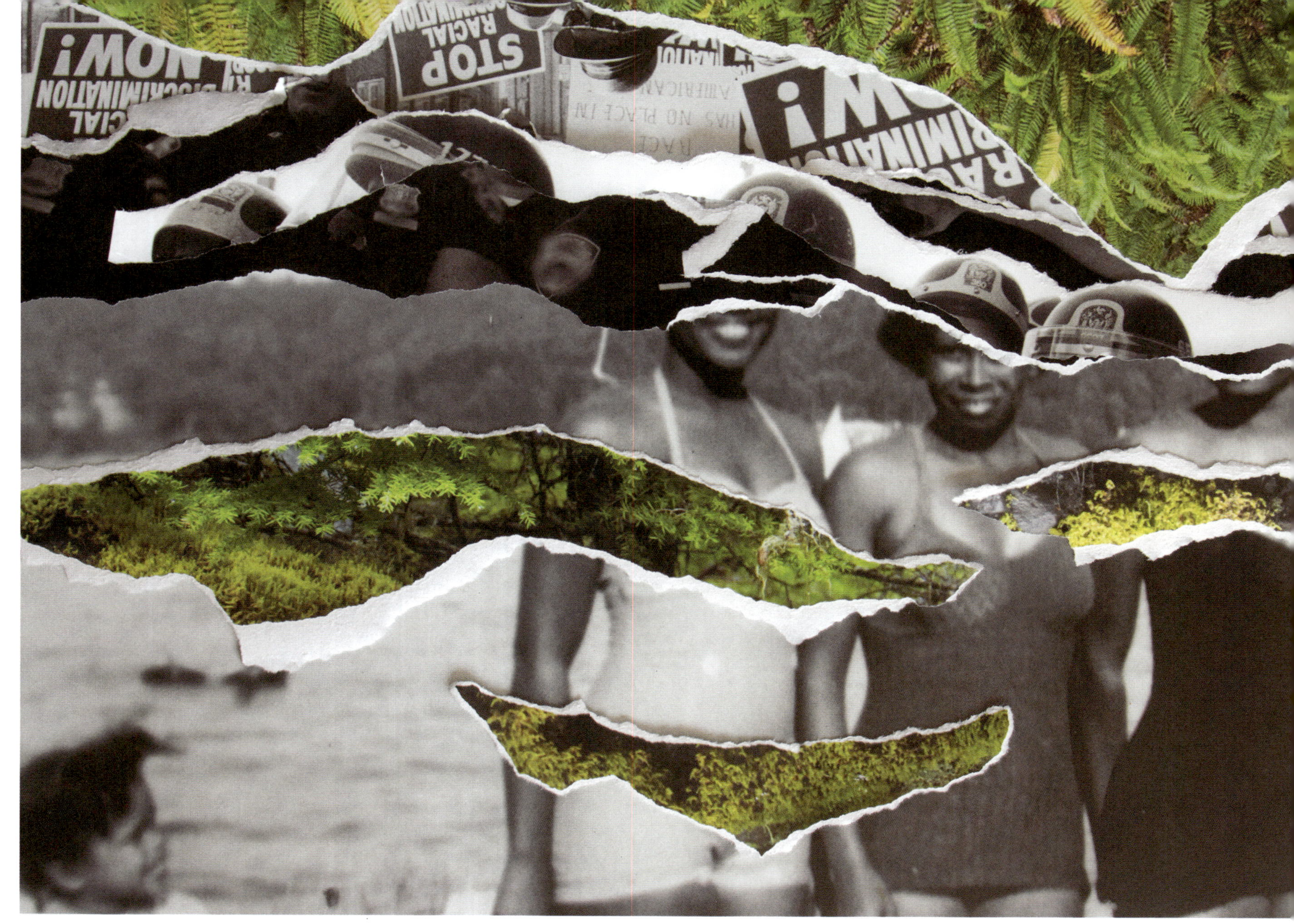

¡NOW!
CIAL DISCRIMINATION
STOP RACIAL DISCRIMINATION
RACE HAS NO PLACE IN AMERICA
¡NOW!
RACIAL DISCRIMINATION

A LOT OF US WERE

just one generation off the farm, if that. That is a reality. You could wander through the neighborhoods and see tall collard greens in everyone's backyard because your grandma, or your auntie, or Uncle So-and-so probably learned how to do that where they grew up.

There was a sense of space just because people lived outside more then. In early summer evenings, we'd just kind of form this big group of kids and dogs and go down to Lake Washington without an adult. A lot of the houses that had fallen down, where Italian immigrants had lived, we used to go and get plums, blackberries, apples, pears even. Or, we would play in the street without an adult because everyone was watching.

The lady who braided my hair, Ms Robinson, was walking distance from our house. I would just walk over and get my hair braided and walk back by myself. Part of the reason it was fun to go over there is because, as a kid, you noticed that older people will act like you're not listening. So I would be in there, and a friend of hers would drop by. And they'd just talk. I would choose a really

INYE WOKOMA
Blue Curtain—What She Saw That Day

complicated, detailed hairstyle so that I could listen to people talk about what's happening at city council, what's happening in the neighborhood, and just kind of soak in some details. I stopped straightening my hair, which caused great consternation with my great-aunt, whose sense of style came about in an earlier era. Of course, in those days we were doing beads. Or you're trying to look like Valerie Ashford from Ashford and Simpson.

After they built the grocery store, at the Promenade, one time, Mom was getting groceries, and I stayed in the car to read a book. There were people and cars around, and then the police were there. They had grabbed a Black man, and they were pushing his arms behind his back. It wasn't so much that he was resisting as that they had twisted him into this position that looked painful and uncomfortable. It was one police officer on each side.

I saw my mom standing with the other people watching. And I heard her call out, "Don't brutalize him. You don't have to brutalize him."

I just stayed in the car and watched because I felt frightened. Mom stayed and talked to the other people who were observing it.

And then, when she came back to the car, she said, "He stole a Mother's Day card."

Zola Mumford

INYE WOKOMA
Blue Curtain—Trouble the Waters

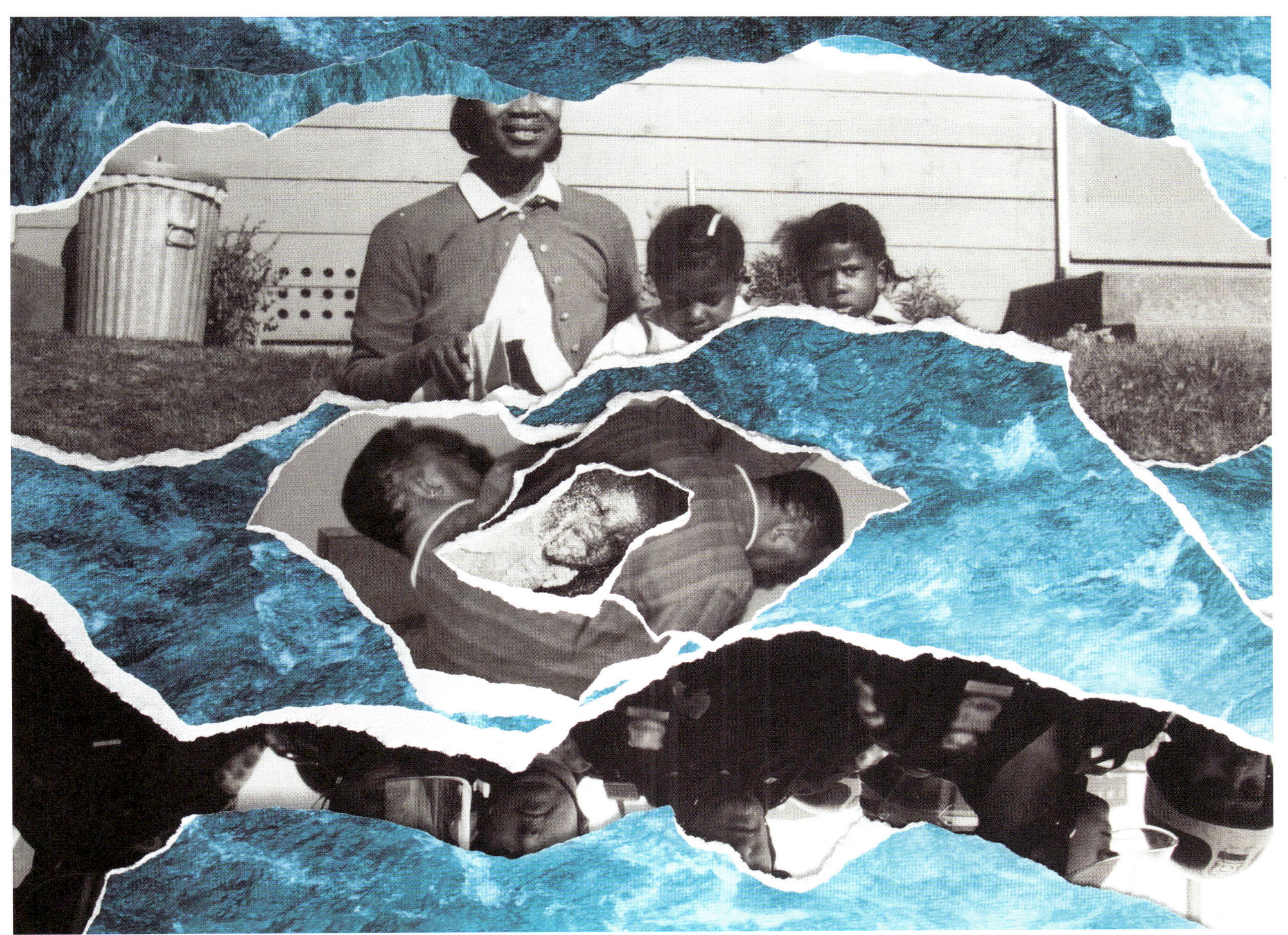

THREE

FAMILY

Over Here

behind the blue curtain
nobody knew what we were doing
the Negroes (that's what we were called
in those days)
of chicago, dallas, philadelphia,
    birmingham
thought it was all trees, bears,
mountains and rain over here
if they thought of here at all
and some did think of here, infrequently
because they had brothers,
aunties, cousins and friends
that wandered off and disappeared
somewhere far off
where Negroes ought not be
but over here
in a small patch of city
we were creating a tiny Black universe
churches, stores, schools,
social clubs, banks, newspapers,
restaurants, night clubs, barber shops
Black labor unions, radio stations
bookstores and community clinics
carved from our memories

Old scrapbooks with saved pieces of home
secreted away in the bottom of suitcases
Fresh letters from distant loved ones
detailing all of the latest
warm newspapers and dispatches
from professional Black observers
working back east
out here, perhaps unbeknownst even to us
the perpetual blue and green
relaxed our organs and our limbs
stretched out our imaginations
the dreams were a little more limber here
because America wasn't looking too
closely
at what a little handful of Negroes
tucked away between two mountain
ranges
were really up to
out here, behind the blue curtain
we created a fractal reflection
of all the places we came from
that also felt like no other place
we have ever been

Inye Wokoma

MY NAME IS

John J. Jackson. Everyone calls me JJ. I was born here in Seattle, Washington, in 1957. I was adopted when I was three years old and raised on 21st and Spruce.

When she adopted me, my mom told me, "You're special, John." I had a skin disease called Vitiligo, which turned me from Black to white. I didn't know where I belonged. I didn't know if I belonged with Black people or white people. Ma was like "Well, you're special, so you're Black. That's the bottom line. You're a Negro."

But I was always straddling the line, you know? When I needed to be Black, I was Black. When I needed to be white, I was white. I knew how to talk white, and I knew how to talk like a Negro. Now, since I've turned all white, when I go into a store, they hurry up and "Can I help you sir?" And I say, "You know, when I had pigmentation in my skin, you never asked me if you could help me. You followed me like I was a thief."

My parents taught me how to survive. I can make soup out of a rock, OK? My mother, Nellie, ran our house. My daddy didn't run nothing, OK? Daddy worked at Todd Shipyard for forty-three years. When he got off work every Friday, he got a check, and he would give the check to my mama. My mama would give him twenty dollars to last him to the next Friday, and that's how it went.

My mama didn't believe in banks. We put money in the mattress. So if we ever needed anything, she had cash. But my mother and father had A-1 credit. We bought a brand new car out of Central Pontiac off the showcase floor. Central Pontiac was there on Broadway and Pike,

DAMON BROWN
JJ

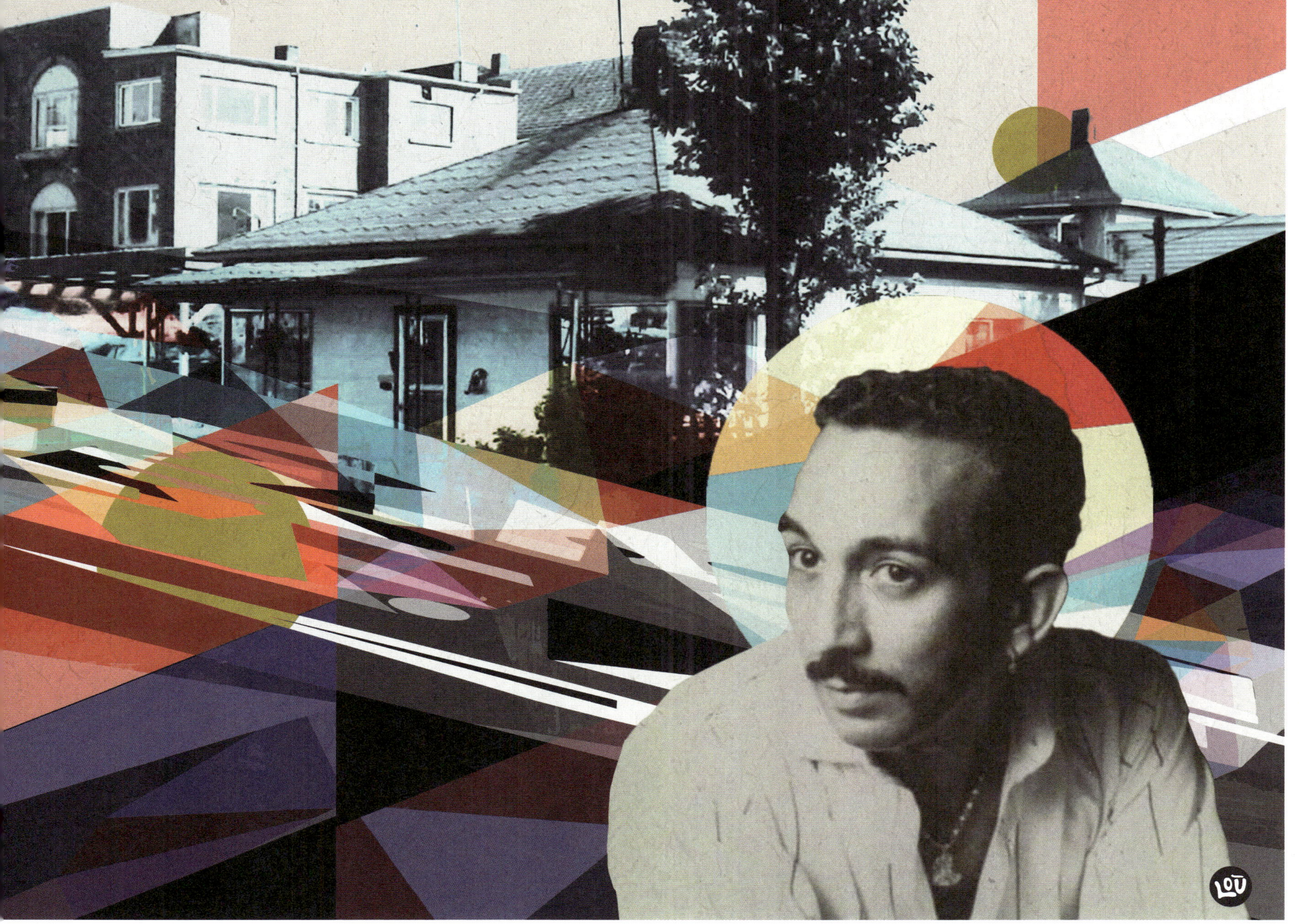

where there's an art store now. My mama bought a 1963 Thunderbird from there, and they tried to sell us one off of the lot, but my mother said, "No. I want the one in the showcase window." And we drove it out of the showcase window. Paid cash. Blue with a white top. "Four doors for four hoes," that's what we used to call it. When Dr. Martin Luther King got killed, Garfield had a riot, and it came across our property on 21st and Spruce. The riot left Garfield and came in front of our house, and they were smashing windows and cars and all that. My mama came out on the porch and said, "You smash something here if you want to, but I'm gonna put a bullet in your ass."

I remember asking mama, "Why are all these Black people running across our lot?"

"It's the Civil Rights movement."

"What is that?"

"It's Black people getting their just dues."

"Does that include me?"

"Yeah, you Black."

My mama and daddy taught me to cook. Mostly my daddy, because my mama, she only cooked twice a year. That was New Year's and Thanksgiving. She made my daddy cook. Even after leaving Todd Shipyard, my daddy would have to cook. He's the only man I know could cook a dinner in thirty minutes. Fried chicken, candied yams, collards, mustard greens. It'd be ready. I named my restaurant after my mother. It was on 14th and Jefferson, Nellie's Place Soul Food and Soul. I opened Nellie's and I started cooking soul food, and people started coming. White people, Black people, all kinds of people. Collard mustard greens, oxtail short ribs, pork chops, fried chicken, pies, sweet potato pie, buttermilk pie, possum pie, red velvet cake, butter pound cake, peach cobbler, six, seven layers. I was there twenty-four hours a day.

MY NAME IS

Isiah Anderson Jr. I was born in Juliette, Illinois, in 1964.

My family are all from Mississippi. My grandmother moved here to Seattle because her husband was stationed here. Then her sister followed her from Indiana.

I came here in November, 1984, to visit my mother and I've been here ever since. She was living on Martin Luther King. It was Black people everywhere. Raising a son here was awesome. There were a lot of Black-owned businesses. The Black Festival was huge here. Lots of food, rides, it looked like a carnival. Exposing my son to all of those things, it was like a family thing.

Every holiday we were at my grandmother's house. She cleaned house all of her life, over in Bellevue and Mercer Island. So her house was always immaculate. She had a runner that went from the front door through the house to the back door, and depending on how long you were going to be visiting determined whether you got off the runner or stayed on the runner. She was the person in the family that everybody bowed down to.

And she would make requests like, "Thanksgiving: Don't bring ya friends, I got enough food for family, don't bring ya friends."

But my brother comes one Thanksgiving, and he's got his girlfriend with him, and my grandmother gets up and locks the screen door. He looks in and he sees everybody, and the whole family knows not to get up and open that door!

He goes, "Hey, somebody come open the door,"

She said, "I wish somebody would open that door."

"Grandma, what's wrong?"

"I told you don't bring nobody."

"Oh, but it's my girlfriend."

"Hi girlfriend. I told you don't bring nobody."

"Oh grandma, quit playin'."

"See if somebody open that door."

So my brother leaves. Five minutes later he comes back without his girlfriend. "I took 'er to the bus stop. I'm not missin' out on Thanksgiving dinner for her."

PHOTO BY
JILL FREIDBERG

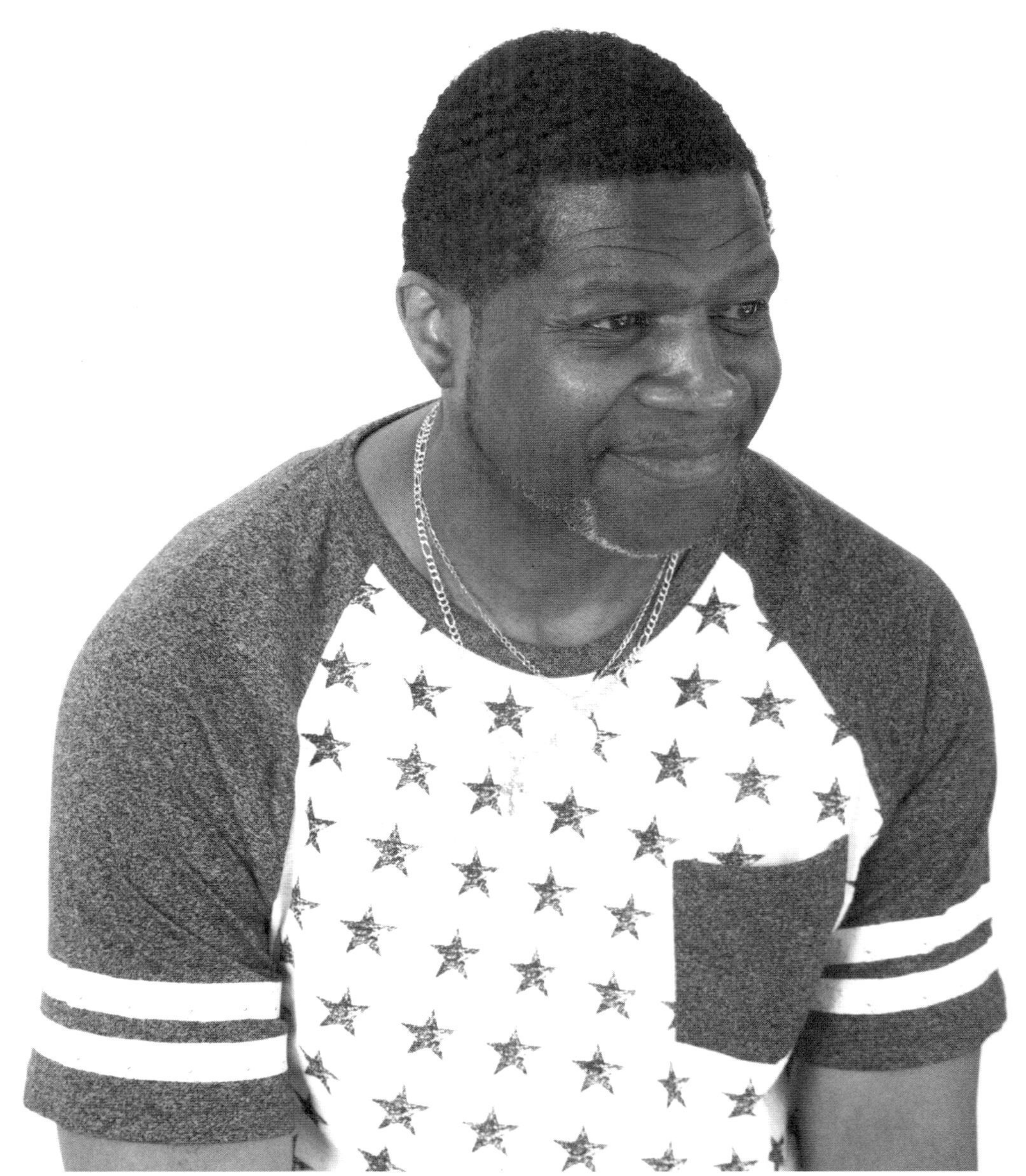

MY GRANDFATHER HAD A BUSINESS

called Scott's Electric. He had like five trucks, they were green and white, and they had a lightning bolt on the side. Whenever that truck passed by, I would go, "That's my family's business." My grandfather and my father were businessmen, and I was really proud of that. I loved my grandfather, he was an incredible man. He had a cousin named Winston who had a farm between Bellevue and Issaquah. My grandfather took me to Winston's farm, put these bottles up on the fence, he gave me a .25, and I knocked all the bottles down. Then he gave me a rifle, and he had me stand further back, and I knocked all the bottles down, and then my cousin's cow walked by, and I asked my grandfather, could I shoot the cow, and he said, "No, no, you can't shoot the cow." I said, "How about just in the leg?" And my grandfather snatched the rifle, and that was the last time I touched a gun.

Gregory Scott

GET TOGETHERS WERE ALWAYS

with my grandmother. She was the one that really held everything and everyone together. Everybody adored my grandmother. She was really funny. She was somewhat strict but with a big heart, and she was just funny. A lot of times we all would end up over at her house, and talk about what it was like when my mom and her siblings were growing up in Texas. My grandparents actually lived in Yesler Terrace for years. Yesler Terrace was really like a playground for kids. We would run all over Yesler Terrace and we would go up to Harborview and make faces at the security guards and they would run us out of the hospital. It was just like a big playfield for us. It was always fun to go to grandma's house, because you knew it was safe to let your kids be out and about as long as they came home when that lamppost came on. I think everybody watched out for everybody's kids. When you hear the stories about if you did something your mom was probably going to know about it before you got home, that's true. That is so true. It is so true. Such a true statement.

KL Shannon

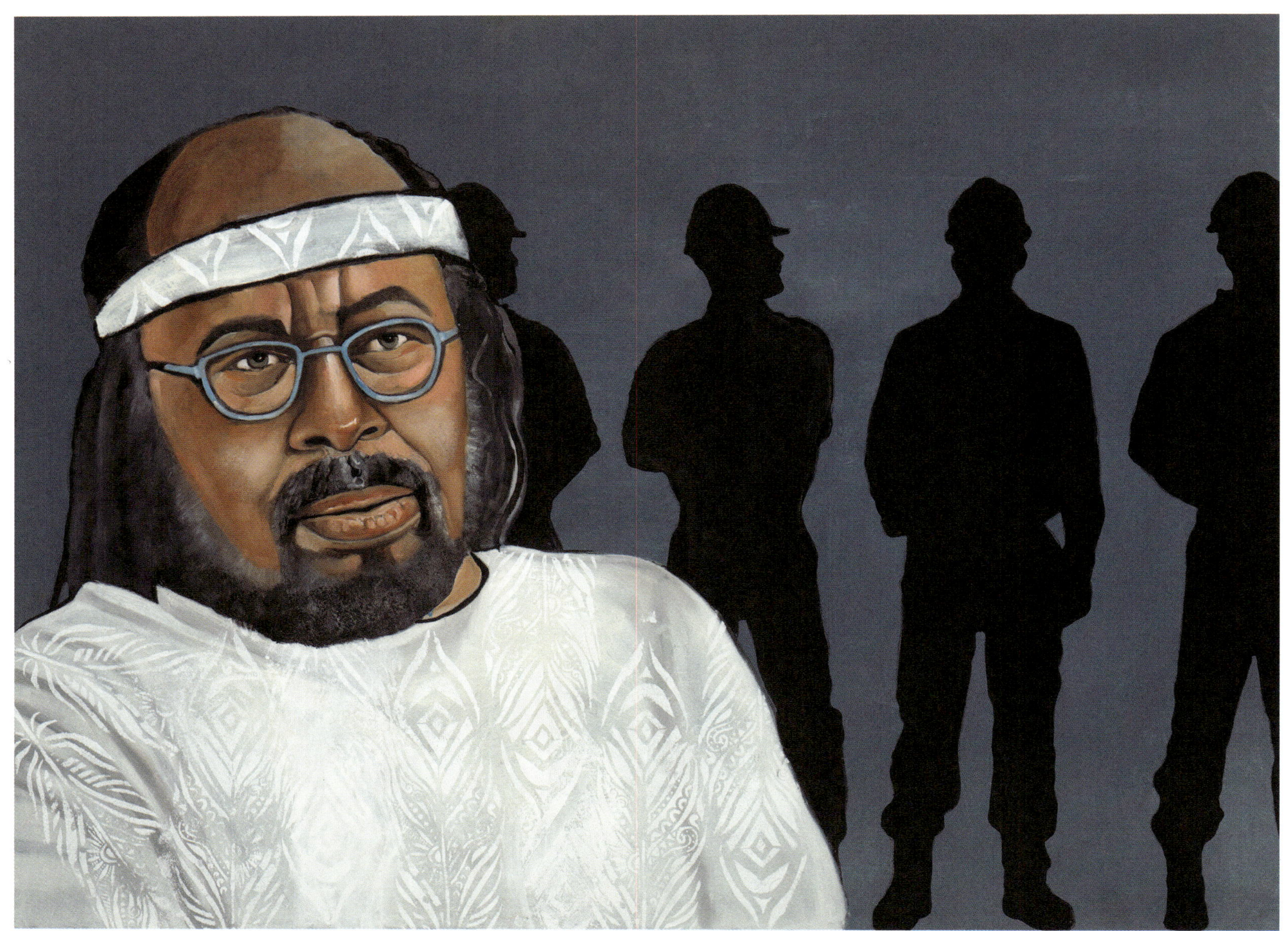

MY NAME IS

Eula Scott Bynoe, and I was born in 1984, at Swedish Hospital, and went back home to the address that I'm still at today, on 26th Avenue.

My Grandfather, Seth Scott, was an electrician here in Seattle. He had an electrical shop on the corner of 23rd and Cherry called Scott's Electric. It was an electrical shop and a bike shop too, one of those really fun neighborhood places where if you were a kid, you went to Scott's to get a bike. And if your bike needed to be fixed, you went to Scott's to get your bike fixed.

What ends up happening though is they're not able to get work. They're all trained electricians. But all the building sites in the Central District were putting just white people on the job. The story is they go to Medgar Evers Pool, and the city is building this pool for Black people, named after a civil rights activist who was shot by a white man, and everybody on the construction site is white. So, they shut it down.

But my dad's history is he shut a lot of things down. My dad is Tyree Scott. So he shut down construction at Medgar Evers; he shut down construction at the University of Washington; they shut down construction on I-90 bridge and the airport and pretty much any time they weren't including people of color on the job.

My dad was a life-long activist, and his main focus was always workers' rights with the mindset that workers rights is all encompassing. His famous slogan was No Separate Peace, we have to all be good for us to really be good.

My daddy had four kids when he met my mom, so they added a floor to our house. It was really built for a party. Whenever we had gatherings, which was all the time, the upstairs was the adults partying how the adults partied, and the bottom floor would be kids playing video games. My parents would have parties, but then they would also have meetings every other Sunday, where people would come over and talk and talk. It was really an open house. It wasn't uncommon for somebody just to walk in and go straight upstairs to hang out with my dad. It was a lot of swinging through. They got down.

BONNIE HOPPER
Untitled

THERE WAS THIS PLACE CALLED

Home of Good Barbecue. On Yesler. They knew my dad when he was young, and from what I remember, that's how my parents met.

My dad told me that my mom was walking across the street, going into the barbecue place.

He was driving his work van. He's going to get bar-becue, and then my dad hits on her from the van like,

"Hey, you're kind of cute."

And my mom was like, "Leave me alone."

And he was like, "Let me buy you barbecue."

And my mom was like, "Okay."

And that's where it all begins.

Sky Sawyer

MY NAME IS

Inye Wokoma, and I was born in 1969, in Seattle. Every Sunday, my Aunt Bertie's house was full. She would go to church at Cherry Hill, and she would come back and start cooking and people would just sort of file through all the way up until the evening. To say that there was always family around doesn't really describe what it was like. On any given day, I could be walking through the community and see four or five relatives just randomly. Not in front of their houses, just randomly in whatever places. There was always family around.

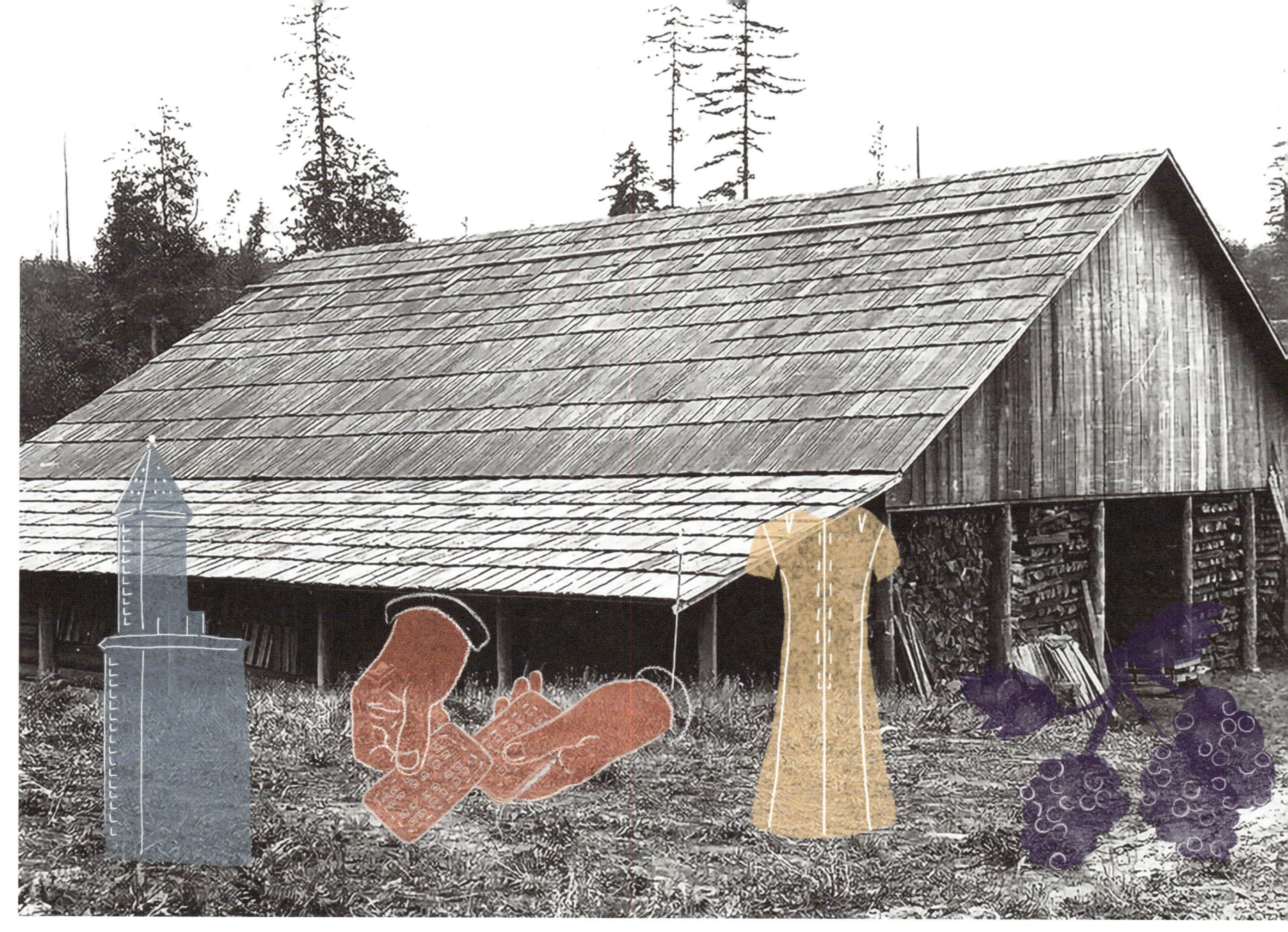

MY NAME IS

Stephanie Johnson-Toliver, and I was born here in Seattle, Washington, 1950. My family came to Seattle as early as 1913. It was my great grandparents, on my grandmother's side, that came here first, from Arkansas. I never have found out the story behind how they acquired property on the south end of Beacon Hill, which back then, was still pretty wooded. They had what I called "the farm" on Beacon Hill. Their home had no lights, no electricity, some chickens, orchards. My great grandfather actually helped to build the Smith Tower.

My mom and dad were divorced when I was about three years old, so I was raised by a single mom whose career was at Boeing for thirty-five years. I probably spent more time at my grandparents' house in the Central Area than I did at home.

My grandmother was an amazing woman, gardener, and seamstress, among 101 other things. She worked at a dress shop downtown, and I can remember going into that shop. All the women on the floor were white women, and then

I'd get ushered downstairs and around the corner and in the back where all the seamstresses were. All Black women, just working away, feverishly, on alterations and whatever else they needed to do. My grandmother loved that place. She actually retired from there. It was called Grayson's, and it was right in that area south of the Bon Marche, or Macy's.

Early in my grandfather's career, he was a card dealer at a club on Madison called Honeysuckles, in the back room. There were a lot of musicians and entertainers that came into town, and they would end up at my grandparent's house. I tried to be the fly on the wall, the little kid sitting there, listening to what's going on, and getting shoo'd out of the room, "Get upstairs, girl! This is grown folk talk!" Their house was a really great hub.

Sunday dinner at my grandparents' was a big deal. Everyone was there. Our whole extended family. It went unsaid. You didn't have to say, "Ok, be sure to show up Sunday, at NaNa and Bompa's." Everybody knew what time to be there, and we didn't bring anything. I mean, there was no such thing as a potluck. My grandma was just, all day, in the kitchen, cooking for everybody. And we actually had the nerve then to get up and walk away from the table. As a kid I don't ever remember washing one single dish. I never participated in the cooking or the cleaning. It was just there. It was fried chicken, mashed potatoes and gravy, greens, yams, the whole works. And, oh, what was really good was this blackberry thing that my grandfather would make called Dandyfunk. We called it that because he would always say "Mmm mmm mmmm this is a dandy funk," the odor of it, when it would cook.

FOUR
ARTS AND CREATIVITY

BONNIE HOPPER
Untitled

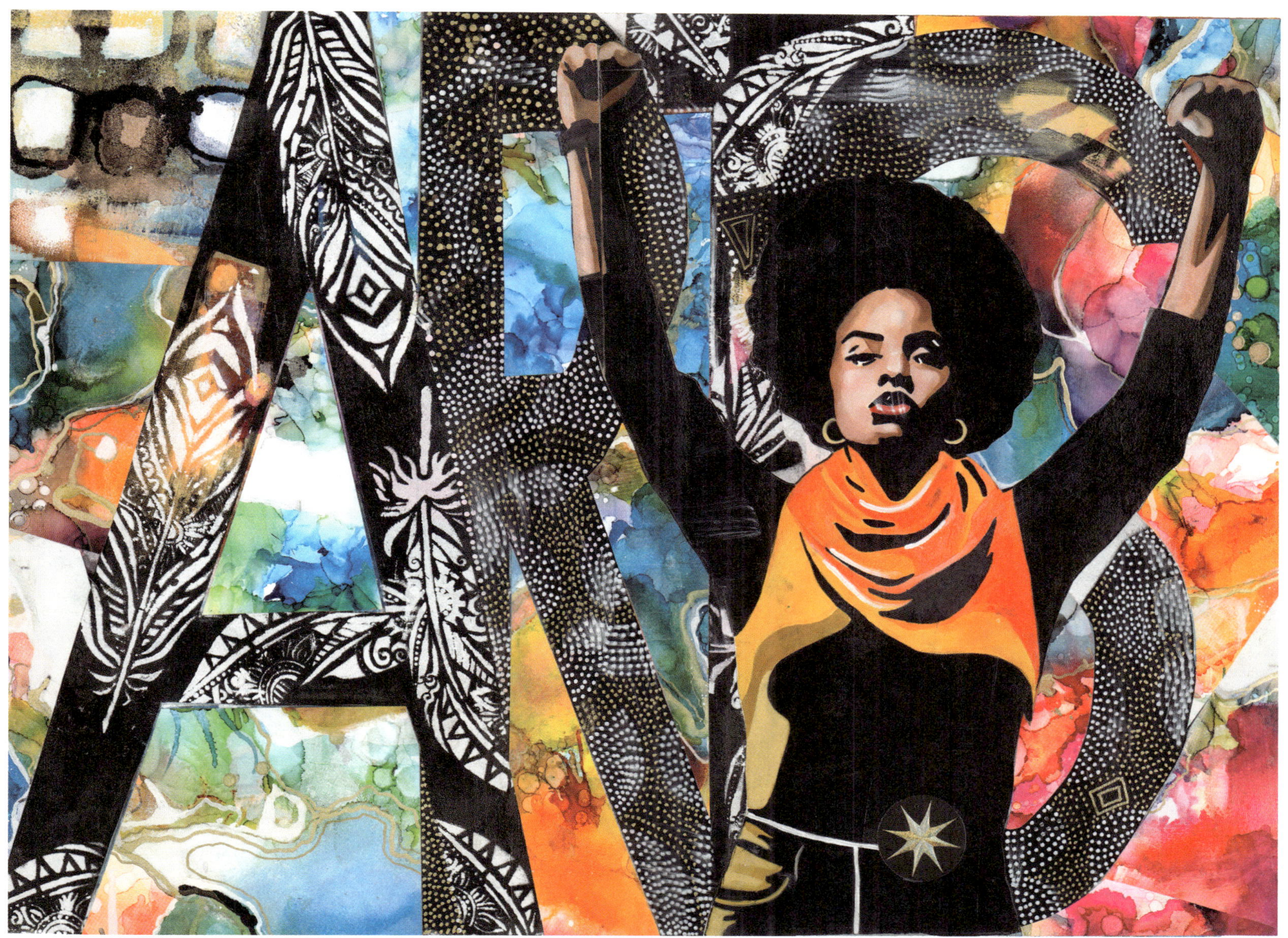

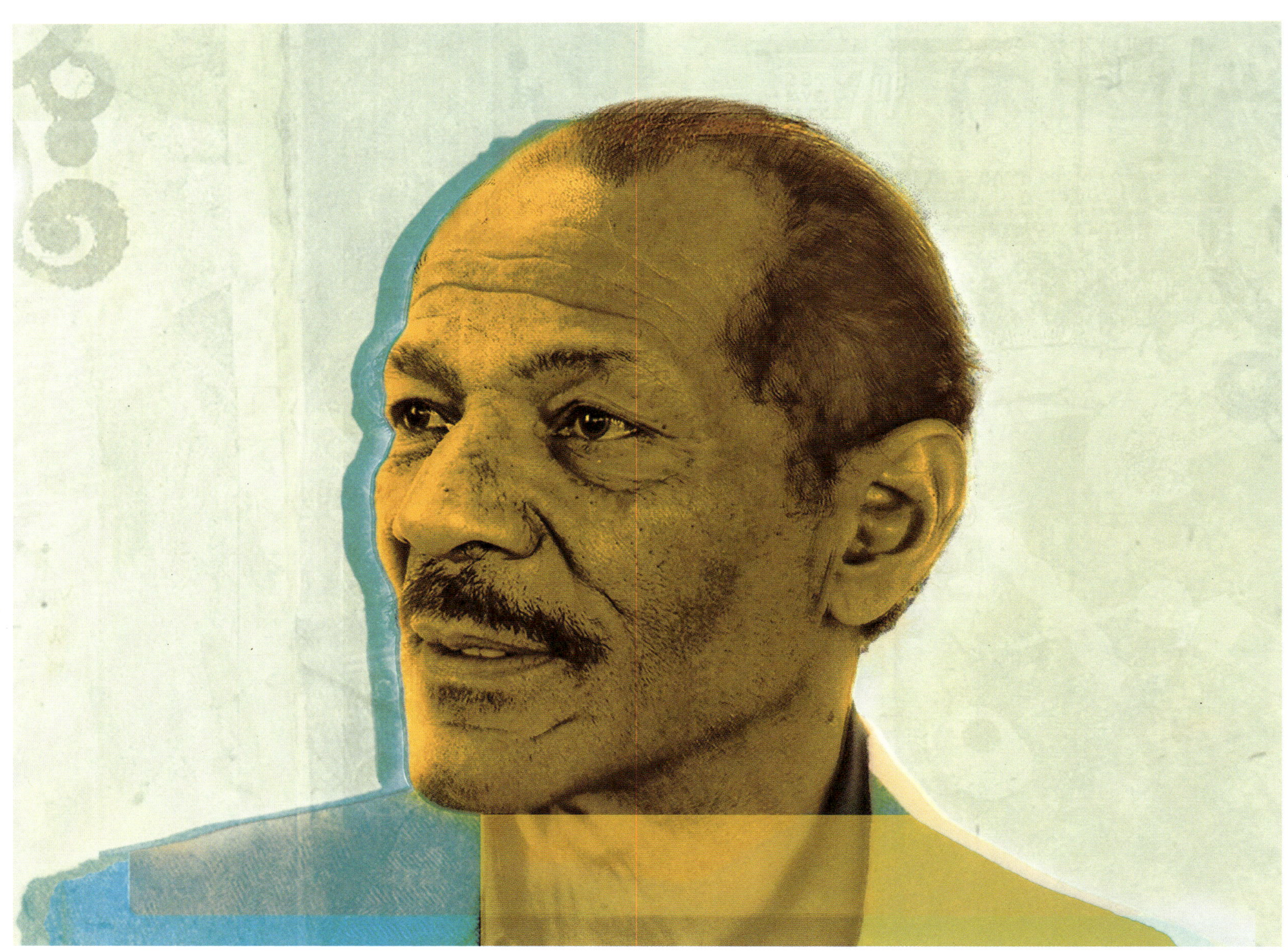

MY NAME IS

Hayward Evans and I was born in 1952, here in Seattle, Washington. My mother, my uncle, a few other relatives, they moved here, in 1946, from Kentucky and from Junction City, Kansas.

I grew up in public housing. High Point, in West Seattle. It was a very close-knit community, a very progressive and supportive community. I didn't realize we were poor until I went to middle school, because the kids who lived in our community all went to the same school. When you got the government cheese or the canned meat, everybody was waiting to get it! On the holidays, we'd get baskets from the Salvation Army, but it wasn't just us, it was everybody.

We always had family members in the Central Area. And one of my best memories is of the Mardi Gras parade. That parade would be right down 23rd Avenue. I was very young, so my mom always would have me at 23rd and Union, amen.

From my observations, the whole founding of SeaFair came right out of the African American community and Mardi Gras.

JITE AGBRO
Hayward Evans

There was a guy named Wilmer Morgan. He had a club up on Madison. He and Lemeul Honeysuckle got together with a few other business owners up on the Madison strip, where all the nightclubs and all the jazz players were. They said, "Let's have a Mardi Gras, like down in New Orleans."

So they started with parades, and every year they had more and more floats, and bands playing. It became a really big deal that attracted everybody out of the city of Seattle. Everybody.

The fact is that it was pre–SeaFair, and I think some of the downtown business community said, "Wait a minute, this is a good idea, let's do something similar." Then they ended up doing a Mardi Gras, then they changed it to SeaFair, and then SeaFair pretty much ignored us. We had one float as an African American community, in SeaFair, and I drove it. Ha!

It was a beautiful float. The Sandpoint Naval Base donated an old landing craft. So we took it up to CAMP, and we didn't know anything about no theme, so we said what would look real nice? Well you know, purple represents the royalty, so we put a purple garland on it, and you know the queen has to sit high! We got one of those big old chairs that the Panthers had, I guess Bobby Seal was in one of them, or Huey P Newton, with the big straw back. We put that at the top of the float. It looked beautiful. We had it all lit up! And we were in the parade. We had queens. In fact our queen came in second in SeaFair, she almost won SeaFair.

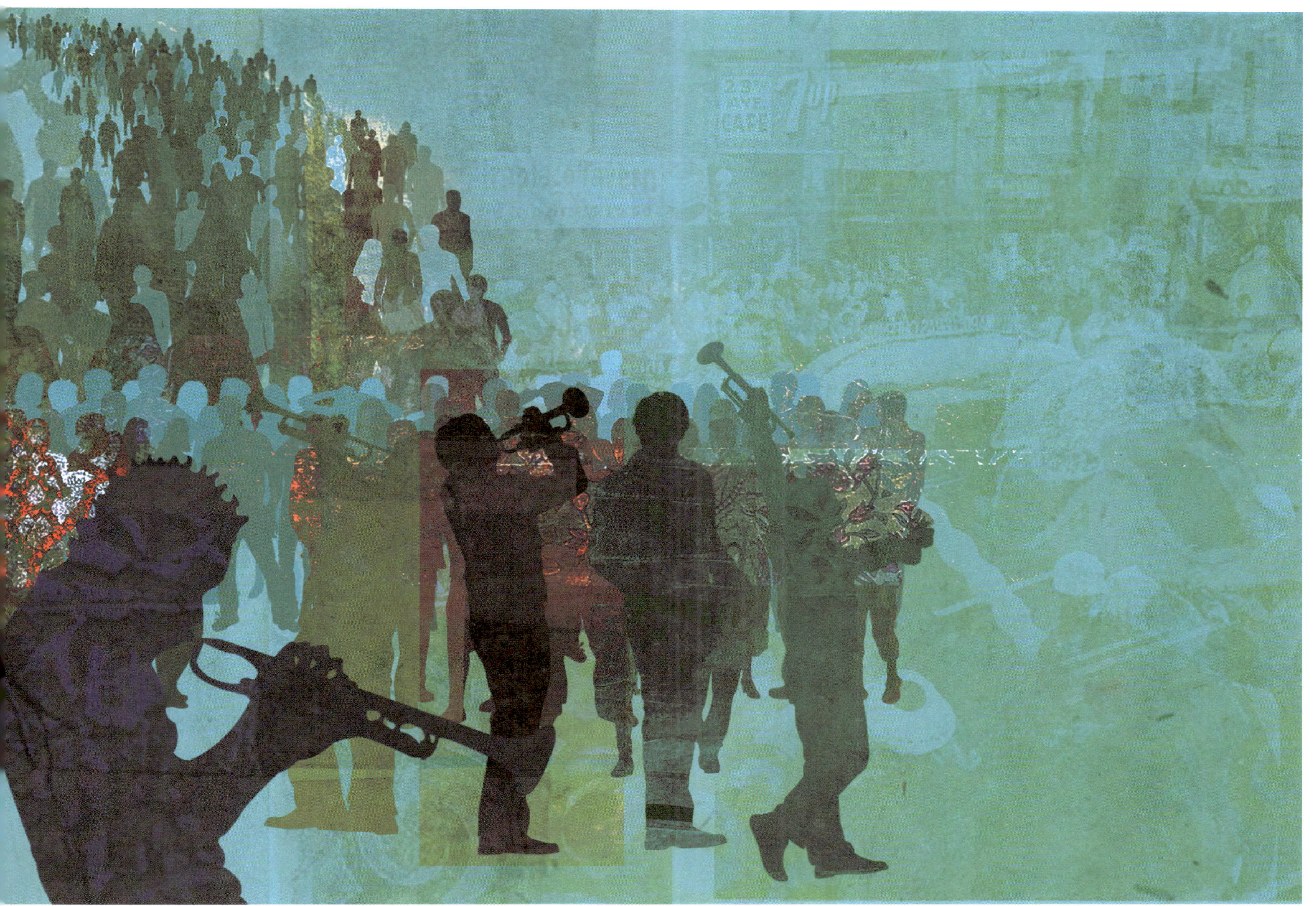
28th
AVE.
CAFE
7up

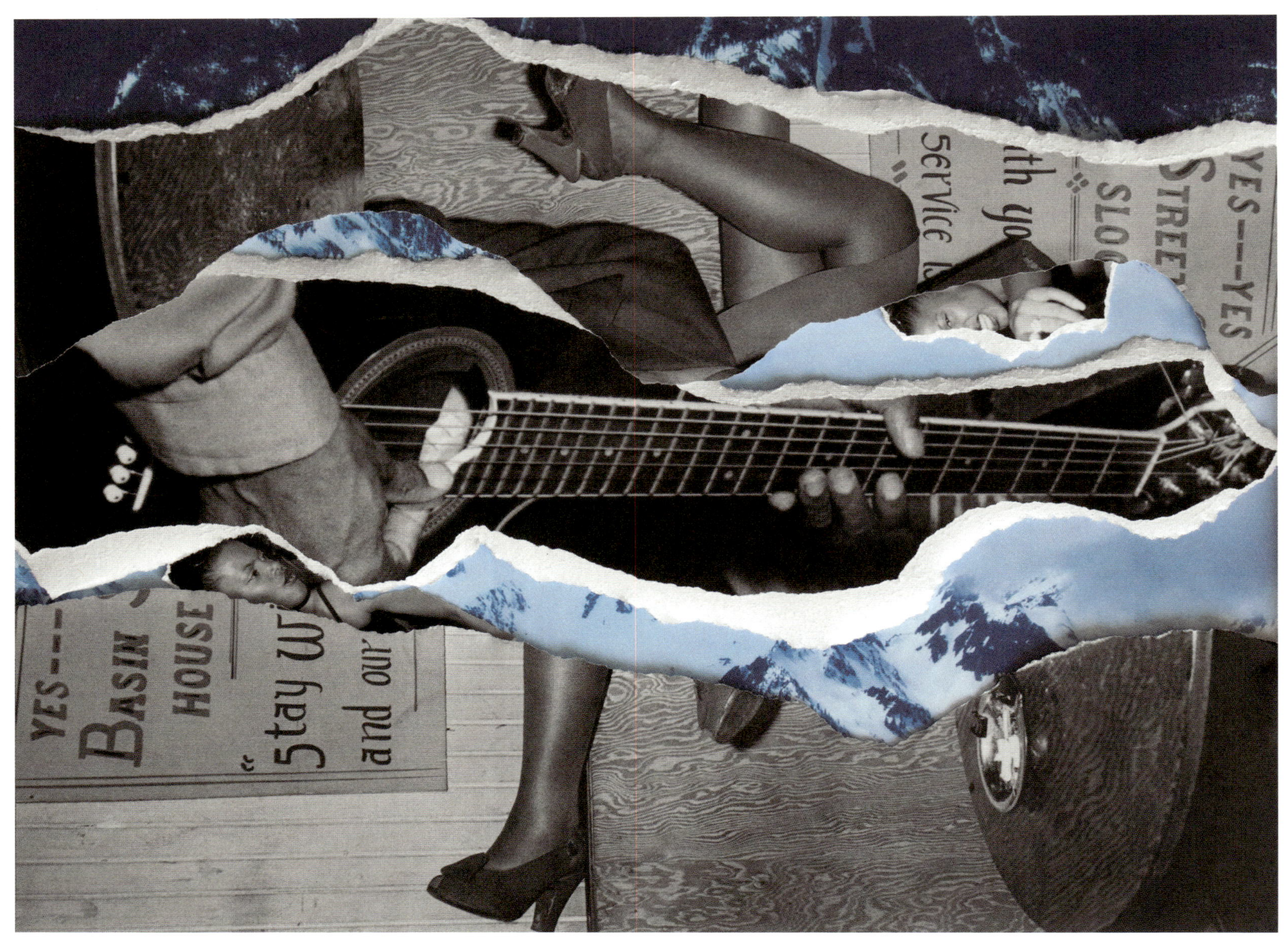

YES---YES
STREET
SLOO
service
th yo
YES---
BASIN
HOUSE
stay w
and our

INYE WOKOMA
Blue Curtain—Paliative Societies

MY NAME IS

Daryl Lockhart. I was born in 1957 and grew up in the Central District.

Our parents came to Seattle from Louisiana. My father worked different places until he landed a job at Puget Sound Bridge and Dry Dock, which later became Lockheed. That's when he was able to, economically, do much better than what he had been doing, to the point where they were able to buy a house. 114 19th Avenue, where we grew up. Our grandmother and grandfather also came up. They bought the house over here on 29th, between Yesler and Fir. And we had aunts and uncles that moved up here too. Uncle Fat came in 1964. Seattle was booming at that time. They were building I-90, and they was building the Viaduct.

We had a family band back in the 70s. Daryl Lockhart and the Rivers of Love.

It started out, I was in the backyard, and I heard some guys banging on some drums, and I went over there to join them. One kid said, "You know what, I got a guitar. Let me go get the guitar." He went and got his guitar. And I remember, "Wait a minute, I actually play the piano. You guys, let's go to my house, and let me play the piano. And bring the drums and all the other stuff with you."

That was the beginning.

The kid with the guitar was Wayne Barrage.

He had been playing in the church for years, like me. He said, "Daryl, I never knew you could play the piano like that. Why don't you join our band?"

The band was called The Gospel Sounds Unlimited. Reverend Maynard, can't think of his first name, he was the bass player. Deacon Flowers was the trumpet player. I was on the organ. Wayne Barrage was on the guitar. We played for the Jesus people, period. They were called Jesus freaks back then. That's what they called them. Coffee houses sprung up all over this city. People was into Christ and you would go to these places and they would serve coffee and donuts and praise the Lord. We played in those places, and didn't get paid nothing. But it was fun.

We hired this white guy as our manager. I don't know why I can't remember his name. That's when we started doing gigs that got paid. One of the last gigs we ever did was at this Catholic Church, St. Joseph's. And it was so funny, because everyone was a Jesus freak then, the Catholic church wanted to kind of update their services, keep people interested. So they hired this band that played basically old school jazz to do a service for them. I'll never forget it. The priest is talking to these people and he's doing aumnni-umumu (impersonates priest murmuring in Latin) and he's doing the cross, and then he turns to us and says, "Hit it!"

And we start tearing it up! In this Catholic church!

Soon after that we decided, OK, there's no money in this and we're going to have to get out of doing gospel music. That's when we changed up and started doing other kinds of music. We competed with some of the biggest bands in the city. They had a Battle of the Bands, five hundred dollars for the best band. We got 250 bucks of that. I mean we had uniforms. We had band practice in the basement. Our dad was our manager. Our mother was our director. We were so young that our parents had to be there as chaperones. But we would do battle with groups like Robbie Hill and the Family Affair, Cold Bold and Together. We played a lot of the military spots, like at Fort Lewis, Bremerton, Sand Point, which was the 456 Club. We had parents that were involved with it and made us rehearse. A lot of musicians in Seattle didn't want to rehearse. They just wanted to show up to the gigs and get paid. My parents wouldn't allow that. You had to come to the rehearsal. We worked a lot of places. We worked all over this city.

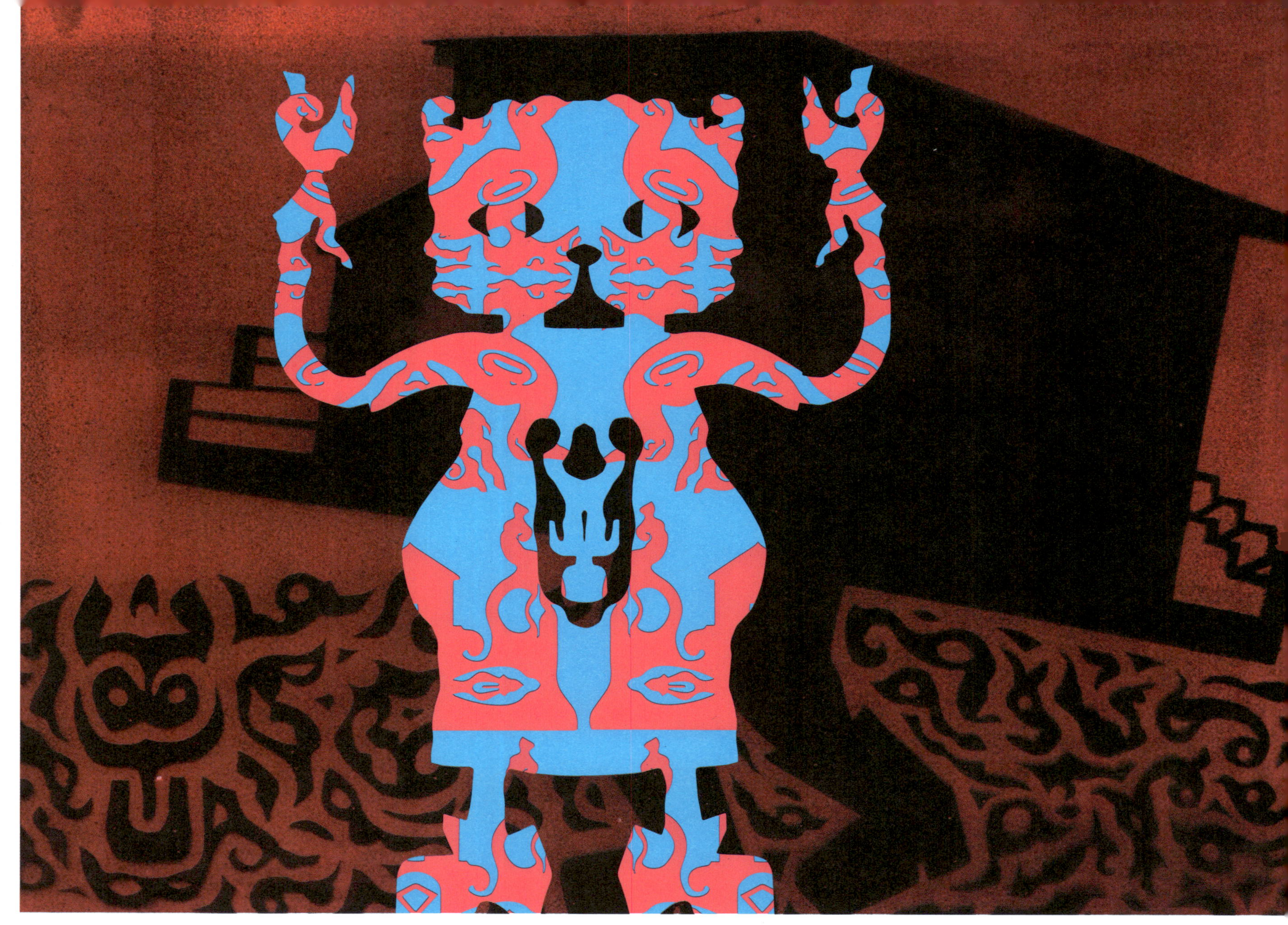

EVERYWHERE THERE WAS ART

I grew up in art. Seattle was an art town. Seattle was an art town that had art apartheid but it was still an art town.

My mother was an artist. She was a jeweler, and she was a part of an art collective called Cicada. They had a gallery on Jackson Street between Eight and Ninth Street, on Jackson, in the ID, so I spent a lot of my time as a child down in Chinatown.

My mother was not into theater, but we spent a lot of time at Black Arts West which was a Black theater group. Al Doggett, who was a prominent artist, my mom, and a few other folks used to hang out at Al Doggett's house and play Scrabble on a regular basis. That is where I learned to play Scrabble. I'm a low-key Scrabble master now. But as a kid, I remember being five or six years old in Al Doggett's house, up here on 34th, and he used to tell us he had some freaking monster in his basement. We used to be scared as fuck to go near his basement door. To this day, I have never been in Al Doggett's basement.

There were way more arts fairs in Seattle and the region than there are now. The University Street Fair, The Bellevue Arts Fair, a regular Arts Fair at Pike's Place Market, an arts fair in Fremont, an arts fair in Kirkland, and Bumbershoot was a legitimate arts place for local artists. Now Bumbershoot is just fucking whatever, it's bullshit. You can quote me on that. My memory of Bumbershoot is it was free, and there were arts vendors,

ROMSON BUSTILLO
Inye Wokoma

it was an arts place. That was the focus. That's what it was about.

And then she would do her art at the Black Community Festival, and we would be there with her. In fact, there were times when there were two arts fairs happening at the same time, and she would register to be at both art fairs, and she would set us up at the Pike Place Arts Fair then go and have her booth at the University District Arts Fair, and my sister and I, she would leave us literally with thousands of dollars' worth of merchandise and she would show us how to fill out the receipt book. We knew how to count the money. We knew a little bit about the art so we could talk a little bit about it. Sometimes she would let somebody know we were down there, and my grandparents might come check on us during the day. And then she would come at the end of the day and we knew how to pack it up, so when she showed up, we just had to get things loaded into the car.

Art was central. It was central to our lives.

Inye Wokoma.

BONNIE HOPPER
Untitled

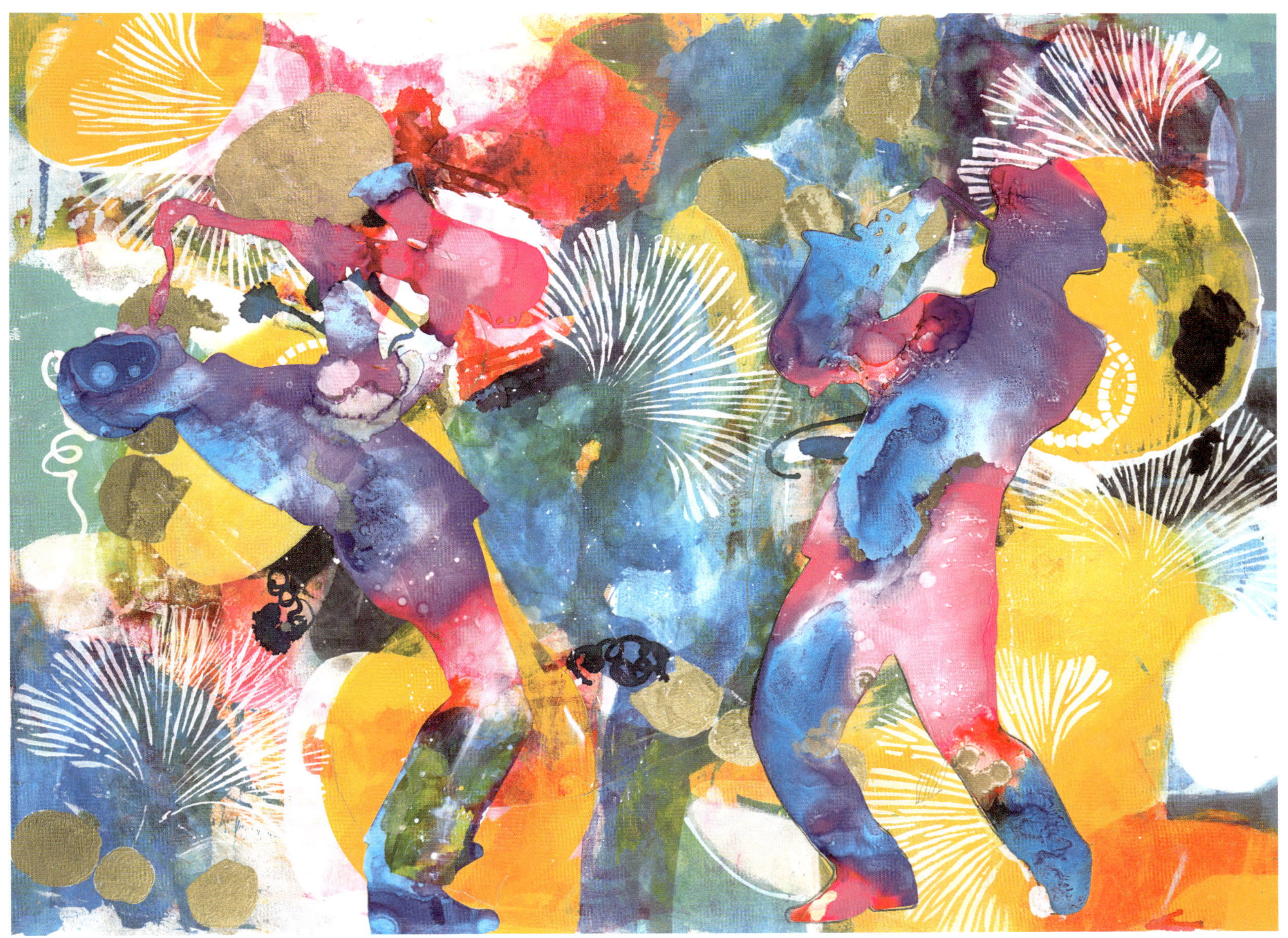

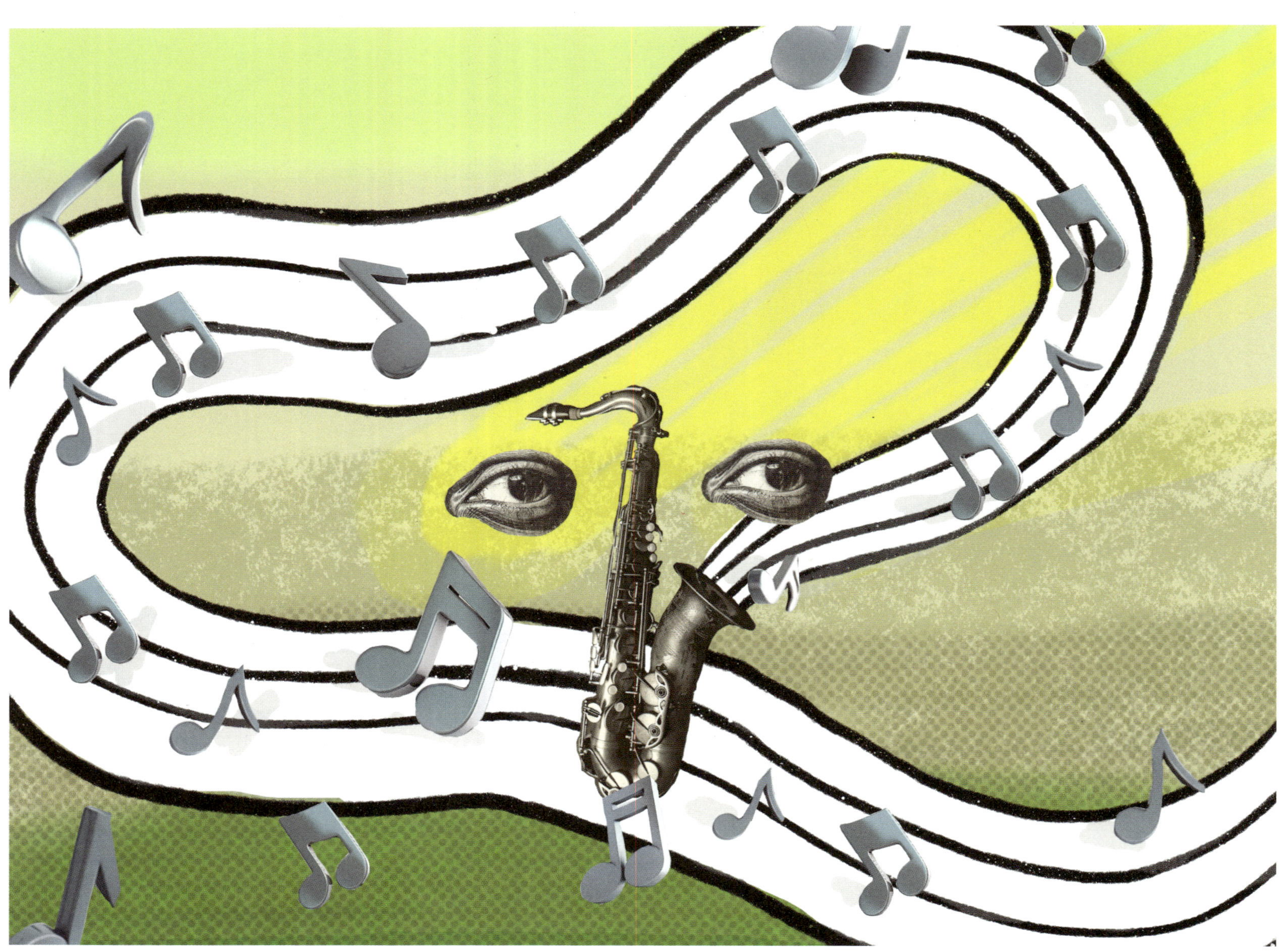

MY NAME IS

Gary Robert Hammon. I was born in Seattle, in 1950. My parents were both from Dallas, Texas. My father had the idea that it was time to move his family from under the Jim Crow regime and bring them to the Pacific Northwest for a better life. He joined the Army and made sure that he got his family to freedom.

Our house was a haven. Larry Gossett's father was the guru for music along with Rocky Woods. They'd have these parties, and there would be music there, and I heard some of the greatest music, I don't care if it was jazz, country-western, whatever, but I heard the saxophone and there was something about that.

I said, "I'm going to play that. I've got to play the saxophone. Wow."

I fell in love with the saxophone. And from then on I've had the bug.

I was in bands. We played for the Masons. We played for the YMCAs. We played for the high schools. We played for the cabarets. We got to the point where we could go into places like 410 Supper Club and Black and Tan. Those were the big clubs, but our groups were good enough. I didn't have to work a job. I played music, see? I made real money. I had a car. My dad didn't buy me a car. I had an apartment. We played in the Blue Post Tavern when I wasn't old enough to be in there, but I'd be in there, because I played in the band, and as long as I kept quiet, did my job, nobody said anything.

CHI MOSCOU-JACKSON
Untitled

MY NAME IS

Stephen David Sneed. I go by Steve Sneed. I was born at Providence Hospital, and I grew up here in the CD.

My dad came first to work in the shipyards. They were from Oklahoma. Dad was from Sapulpa. Mom was from Tulsa. Dad went to a Black college down there called Langston University. But his dad told him a Black man can't earn a living going to college. "That's a waste of time, getting an education. You need to get a job like a real man and work in the brickyard," which was close to there. But my dad was born in a time when education was really important amongst young people. I mean, it was revolutionary to get an education. So he got the education anyway. But he couldn't make any money. He wanted to teach English and write books. And he couldn't get paid well enough. So, somehow he found out about shipyard work up here. And he came up here and worked in the shipyard during the war. And then he went back to bring his wife out here. Coming up here for them was...it was a place where a Black man could just have a family, be paid decent for his work, and move about in the city.

DAMON BROWN
Steve Sneed

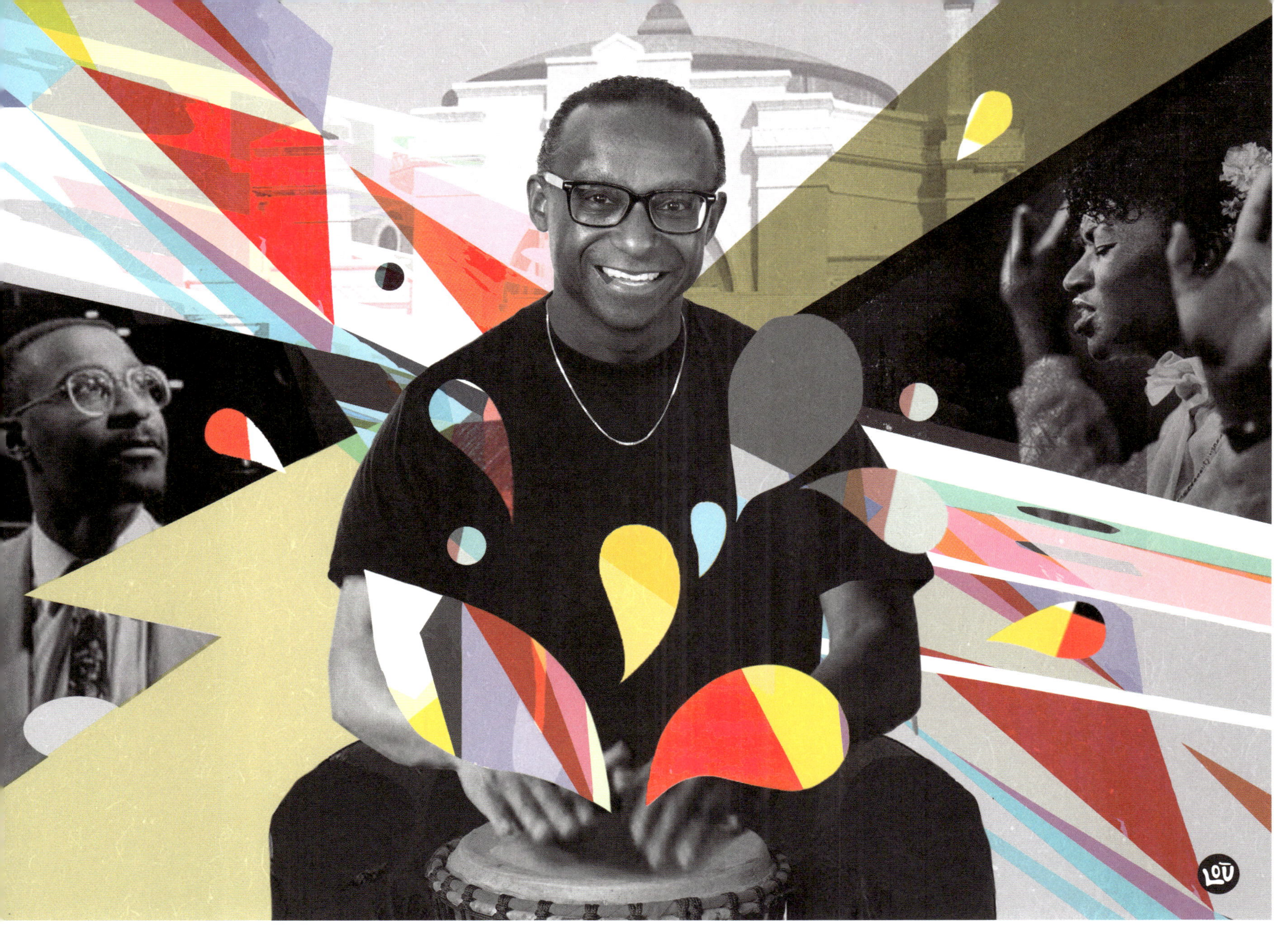

When I was a teenager, we had an African drum and dance group. I played the drums. In the '70s, the African drum and dance thing, for high school kids, was like hip-hop today. Everybody wanted to do it. Everybody was doing it. We were kids, you know. We played all over. We had no adult supervision. We did this totally on our own. We started at fifteen years old. But we did have some teachers. We had some African drummers come in and show us how to actually play the drums.

Our claim to fame was that we played every prison in the state of Washington. I mean, every single one. Walla Walla, Monroe, Purdy, and not just once. We'd go regular. Every year we'd go back to Monroe. The Black community festivals, of course, we'd always play every year. We'd play churches. Seven years we did this consistently, rehearsed regularly through the week.

The unique thing about our group was we played African rhythms, but we had some modern instruments and we also wore costumes that were like a combination of Sly Stone and an African drum and dance group. We had glitter.

My sister, who was younger than me, wound up doing comedy at about thirteen. She performed at some of the festivals and she was really funny. So she started working at Black Arts/West. I went to all the plays back then and was just starstruck. But the first audition I went to, I never made it because I was so scared. I turned right around. It wasn't until I got to University of Washington, Black Theatre Project, I was doing a play every quarter. I got over the fear. I ended up doing the very last play at Black Arts/ West, which was Brownsville Raid. I did that play. And we performed it at the University of Washington.

When I left the University of Washington, I got some plays at the Children's Theater and ACT and The Rep. I was immediately placed in the union, first play I did. This was just finishing college, in '79, '80. I was still broke, because I was an actor. But I got a job at the Boys and Girls Club where I started what was a youth theater. Myself, Reco Bembry, and also Darcell, we all came from the African drum and dance group and started this youth theater with a DCM approach: Discipline, Confidence, Motivation. The idea was to teach young people, not just to be actors, but to learn how to function in life, to build some character traits.

But then Reagan was elected. So they cut the funds and I didn't have a position at the Boys and Girls club anymore. I don't think I worked there even a year. Meanwhile, the Parks Department was ready to tear down the Langston Hughes building. This is the '80s. The building is empty. Nobody's using it. The kids are almost afraid to go into the building, right? So I joined the advisory council at Langston Hughes and then got a position there, assistant recreation coordinator. More youth theater. Parks thought

this was wonderful, a summer musical program, young Black kids doing something positive, right? They were so elated they moved Bev Harkey out of leadership, and they put me in the lead spot. We did plays. We taught kids filmmaking. There were people in the building again.

PHYLLIS:

Daddy sang in a men's chorus acapella called the Song Crafters by Joseph Powe. They did a play with a company from New York at the Greenlake Aqua Theater. Between the stage and audience was a big body of water, and it was the aqua theater.

Cecil: What Joe Powe did there was put members of different choirs with our men's chorus, to have one huge choir. He had this guy from New York with a real deep bass voice, and he sang Old Man River, and we sang the background music to it, and in the swimming pool the girls did their synchronized swimming. It was really a big show.

Phyllis: My parents were in the chorus, so I went to rehearsals with them every day. I knew every line, every song, every move on that stage.

One day the director said, "We need some Black kids, bring the Powe kids down."

I said, "The Powe kids?!"

Mr. Powe had like four kids.

I threw a fit.

I fell out screaming, crying, desperate to be on that stage. My mother knew nothing was wrong. She didn't move.

But Daddy came up there, 'cause he couldn't stand to see us cry.

I said, "I want to be on the stage! He asked for the Powe kids!"

And Daddy said, "You just as po' as the rest of them, go on down there!"

I jumped up and ran down to that stage! I knew what he said didn't make a damn bit of sense, but if it got me on that stage, I didn't care. And the guy didn't know a Powe kid from a non Powe kid, so he put us all in the show.

Phyllis Yasutake and her father Cecil Beatty

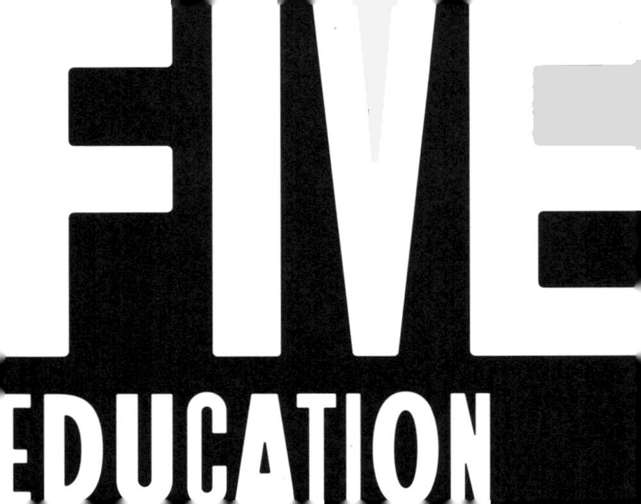
FIVE
EDUCATION

When we were conducting Shelf Life
interviews, most people talked about
two things:

1.) The importance of school being close
to home, so that parents could go to the
school and intervene every time their
children were disrespected, forced to read
racist books, or forbidden to read Black
writers; underestimated, overlooked, or
subject to punishment disproportionate
to the crime.

2) The importance of non-traditional
educators: mentors, coaches, artists,
someone else's mom, librarians, cross-
ing guards, barbers and beauticians, the
people who saw and fostered potential in
ways the public schools never would.

*Phyllis Beatty Yasutake, and her father, Cecil Beatty,
were interviewed together.*

MY NAME IS

Phyllis Yasutake. I grew up in the
Central District.

My parents came here in the early 40s. My
mother came from Little Rock, Arkansas. And
my dad's from Oklahoma.

My dad was a machinist, and he went to work
in the shipyard, and my mother came here
through a program for young women that had
them living in a dormitory and working in the
shipyard offices.

I spent a year out in the north end, as the
only Black kid at Woodrow Wilson Elementary
School, because my aunt and uncle needed
me to live with them to babysit, and I never
wanted that experience again. So I picked
Franklin High School because I knew Black

people at Franklin. I wasn't gonna be the only
one ever again.

I was in band, and I played flute and piccolo,
and my dad came to all my concerts. He'd
sit in the front row and have his reel-to-reel
recording everything and he'd sleep.

They'd say, "Isn't that your dad?"

"Yeah."

"Isn't that him sleeping?"

"Yep, but he's right there. Where's your dad?
Is he here? Well mine is here."

BONNIE HOPPER
Untitled

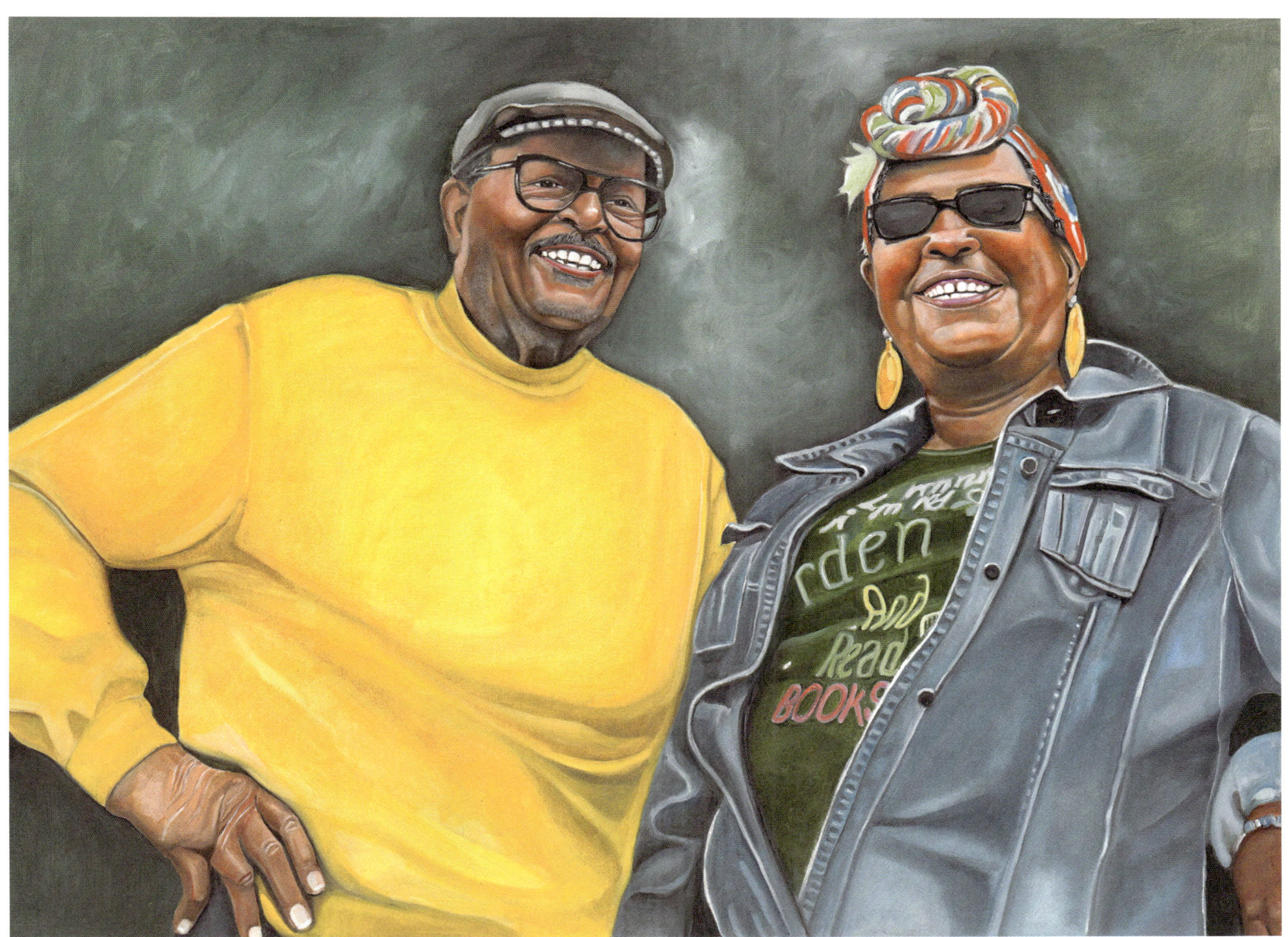

rden
Read
BOOKS

Cecil: She was very smart. She's got a photo-graphic memory. But she made straight Fs in school.

P: Not straight Fs, Daddy.

C: What the teacher was trying to teach was boring to her. Anyway she was down at Franklin, and the girls were fixing the runs in their hose with fingernail polish. When they passed it to her, the teacher put her out of class and put her in a study hall. This was an algebra class. I found out and I went down there and talked to the assistant principal. He gave me a lot of lip, and I said, "I tell you what, my wife is Secretary of the NAACP..."

P: "...and your lawyer is President of the NAACP, and your brother-in-law is the Chairman of CORE."

C: I said, "Within thirty minutes I'll have so many people down here picketing this school it'll be so hot for you that you'll have to go up to Alaska to cool off. There's gonna be a Beatty in that algebra class. You can put her in there, or you'll see me and about half a dozen NAACP members in that algebra class. Your choice."

He went in and said something to the princi-pal. Next thing I know they yanked her out of that study room and put her back in the algebra class.

I went down to that school so much, one of the kids down there asked me, "What class do you teach? I've never been in your class."

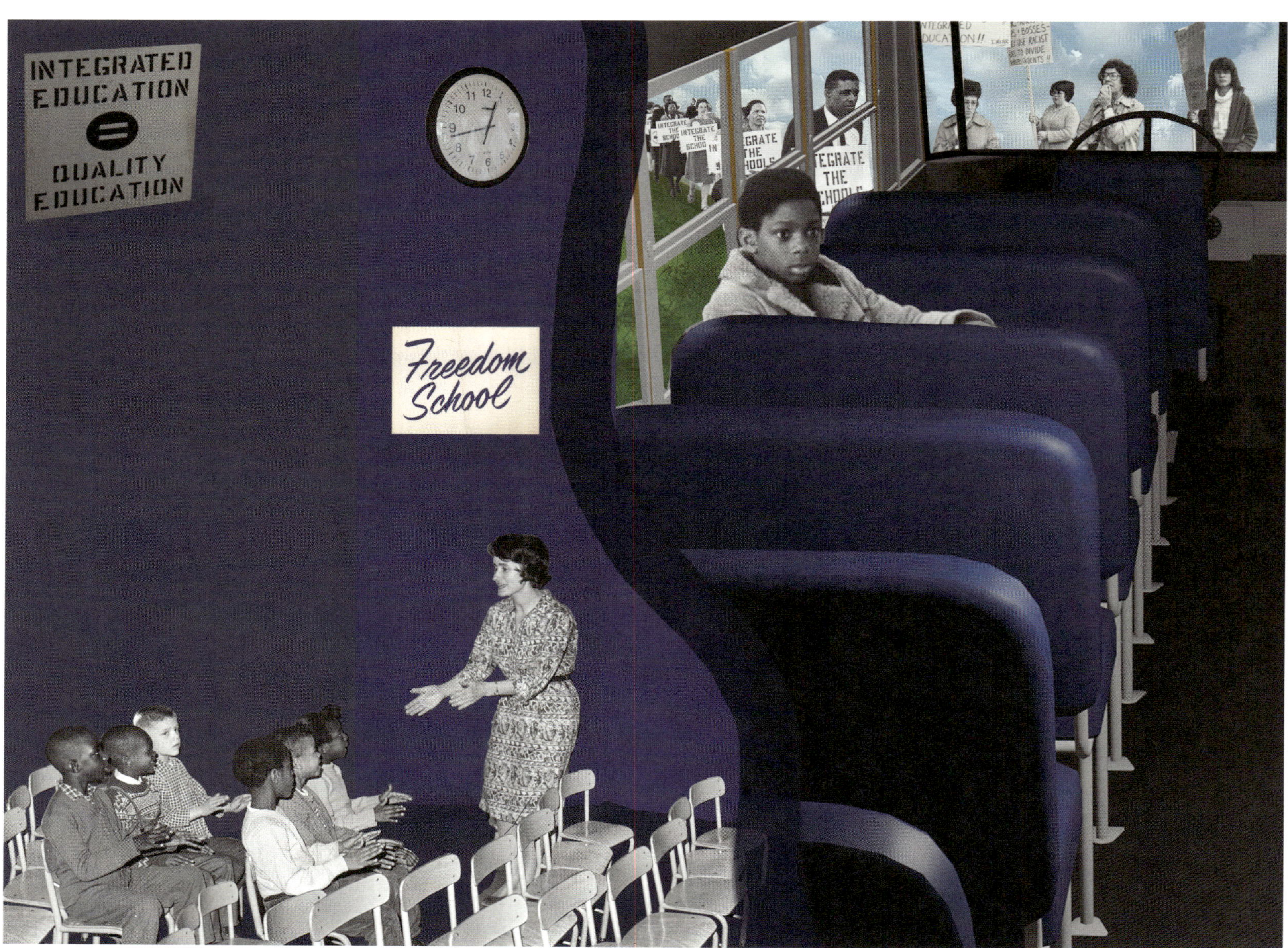

INTEGRATED
EDUCATION
=
QUALITY
EDUCATION

Freedom
School

INTEGRATE
THE
SCHOOL

INTEGRATE
THE
SCHOOLS

INTEGRATE
THE
SCHOOLS

INTEGRATED
EDUCATION!!

THERE WAS A SCHOOL BOYCOTT

This was led by the Black churches, Mount Zion, First AME Church. There was an effort to allow Black children to go to schools in other neighborhoods because the thinking was that our schools in the Central Area were subpar. Young teachers would come in, get trained, and then they'd move them out. Black parents just wanted the opportunity for their kids to be able to go anywhere.

They were right about the education part of it, but they were wrong in terms of what happens if you send everybody out of the neighborhood schools.

Anyway, they boycotted the schools. They took two days. All the Black children came out of the schools, actually some white children as well, Asian children as well, all came out of the public school system within the Central Area. And they had freedom schools. They took the kids to churches and community centers and did Black history education. It made such an impact that the school system then started the process which ended up being busing.

CHI MOSCOU-JACKSON
Untitled

That busing, culturally it was hard on people. It was so difficult for me to come out of Horace Mann and go to BF Day for fourth, fifth, and sixth grade. By sixth grade, I said, "I've got to go back." At BF Day, it was like I was in a hole or something. There were no good experiences that I can remember. I was all alone. I'd bus out there, and it seemed like an eternity. It seemed so far away. When I finally did go back to Washington Middle School, it was depleted. But at least, my mother could come to the school. She would be in the hallway and stuff. My older sister taught one of the classes there. So it was much more community, right?

There was this one bus monitor when we were being bused out; tall, Black man. He always wore a long, black trench coat, black slacks, black shoes, black hat, to monitor the bus. He was dressed clean. I think he had a tie on, too. But I remember he said something about me being a leader. And I was thinking, "What is he talking about?" I'm in fourth, fifth or sixth grade, right? But, I never forgot he said that.

Steve Sneed

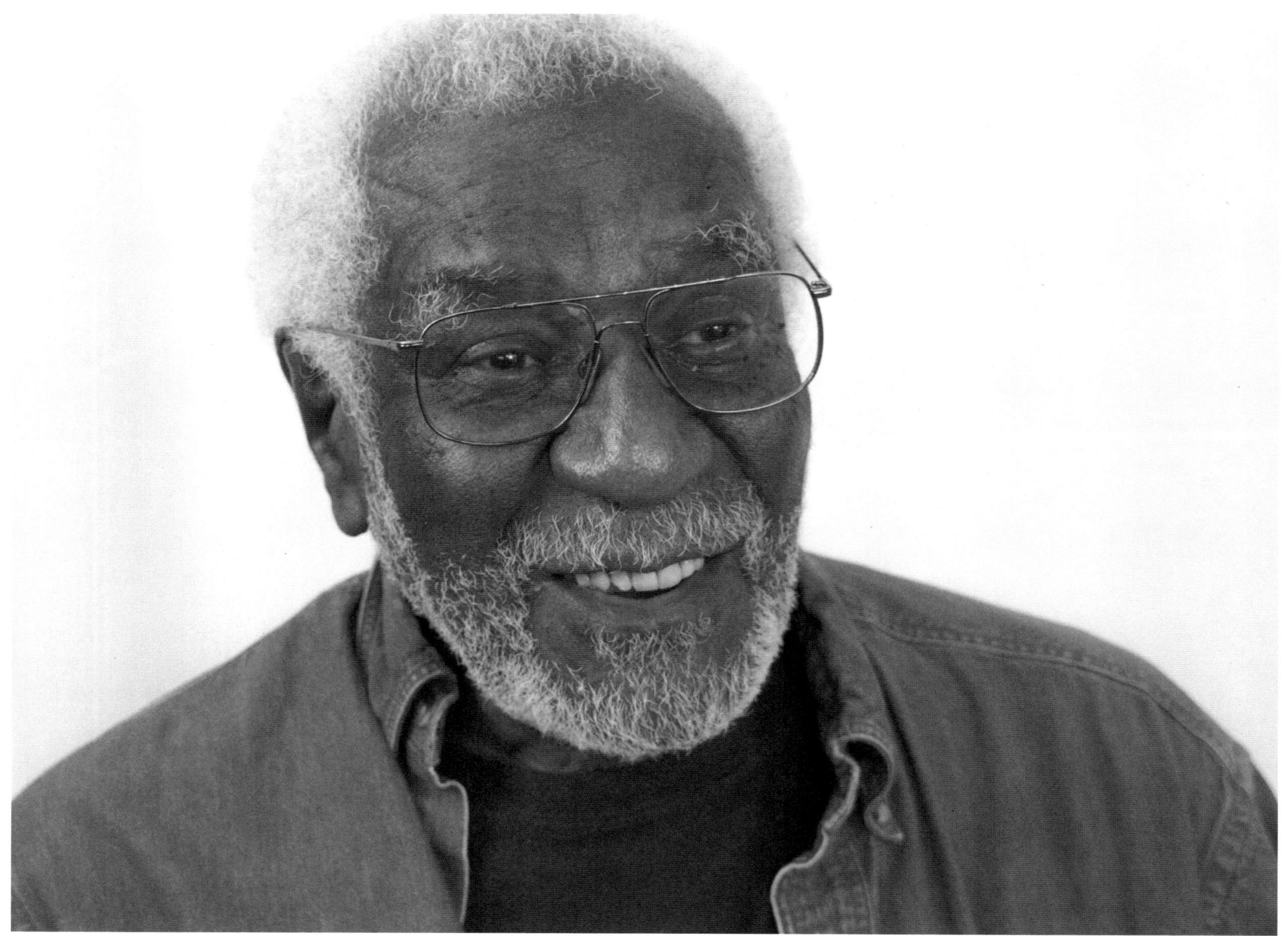

THE SUNDAY NEWSPAPERS

We'd read those all together, the cartoons especially. They even had these radio stations that read the cartoons on the radio, so we'd read along with them, and that's how I really learned how to read. When we were introduced to the library as kids and told we could pick out any book we wanted on the shelves, I really got into stuff beyond just little children's stuff. I got into big children's stuff.

This is all before I even went to school, so when I went to school, I was a little ahead of all the other kids. It was a bad experience, by the way, just knowing too much. I went to Horace Mann. I was in the first grade, and they boosted me from a 1B to a 1A, because I could read really well. One day the teacher had people getting up in front of the class and reading out of a book. It came my turn, and I was reading, and I ran across a word I didn't know, and she grabbed me and shook me, and I started crying, and she put me over her leg and started spanking me, and I just bit her in the leg, so that was the first school I ever got kicked out of, Horace Mann.

There were books that my mother didn't allow us to read, like Tom Sawyer and Little Black Sambo, stuff like that. But sometimes they'd read them in school, and our mother would go straight to school and tell them. When I was in grade school in South Park, my mother came down and talked to the principal and said, "If they ever read those books in class, my children can get up and walk out." Most of the schools at that time were predominantly white, and she was pretty strict about racism. We weren't allowed to call people certain names, even during the Second World War. We weren't allowed to call Japanese "Japs." We'd get the bap-a-lap, as she called it. A spanking!

Mark Cook

I WENT TO

Colman Elementary, Washington Junior High School, and Garfield High School. Maxine Mimms was a sixth grade teacher at Colman Elementary. My class was in the portable next door to Ms. Mimms' class, and she was an incredible role model. She wore suits and high heels every single day, every day. She's the woman that I tried to emulate when I became an adult. She didn't care if you were in her class or not. She knew that she was an African American female role model for all those kids and so she was the safe person we could go to regardless.

I got kicked out of school for having an afro in eighth grade. You know my mom was mad, because that Sunday she had spent all day pressing my hair. She had been sweating and pressing hair for hours, and I immediately went and got it whacked and went to school with an afro.

One white teacher at Garfield, Sally Pangborne, took a group of Black kids, and she told us the truth, and she taught us from these radical books. And they fired her. She was fired because she felt it was important that we knew more about who we were. So when they fired her, she invited us to come to her house, and she taught us at her house, and then they reinstated her.

I wasn't the best kid. I didn't get in trouble a lot, but by the time I was fifteen or sixteen years old, it was on. I joined the Panthers and all that. I was out in the streets, you know, trying to be grown. I bored easily and I picked up information really quickly. I didn't feel like I had to go to school five days a week. So they sent me to Nova, and that's where I learned art. Dion Henderson was my art teacher, but by the time I was a junior I was like, "Okay I really can't come to school five days a week."

One of the counselors said, "What do you like to do?"

"I like to sew."

So they put me in this program, Blues Illustrated Boutique. A group of us who were highly skilled at sewing made all the clothes that were sold in the boutique. Ms. Lindsay Mackland was the teacher there. She would make the patterns and cut it out for us and we sewed that stuff up. We'd do fashion shows all around the community and sell our clothes. It was Ms. Mackland that wrote in my yearbook that I had "the depth of perspective, and the skill, to succeed," and that changed my life. It changed my life.

Vivian Phillps

ERIN SHIGAKI
Untitled

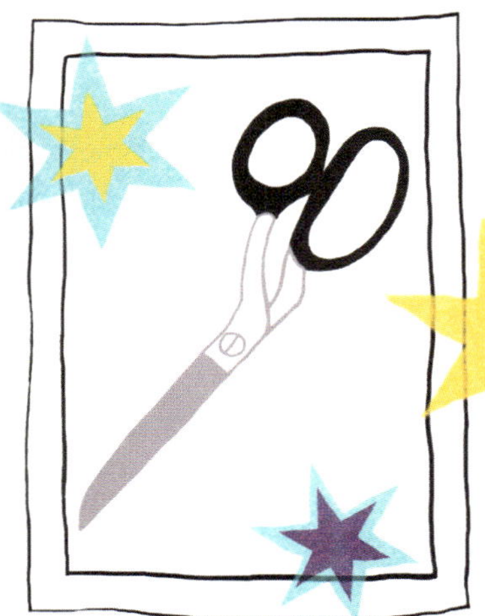

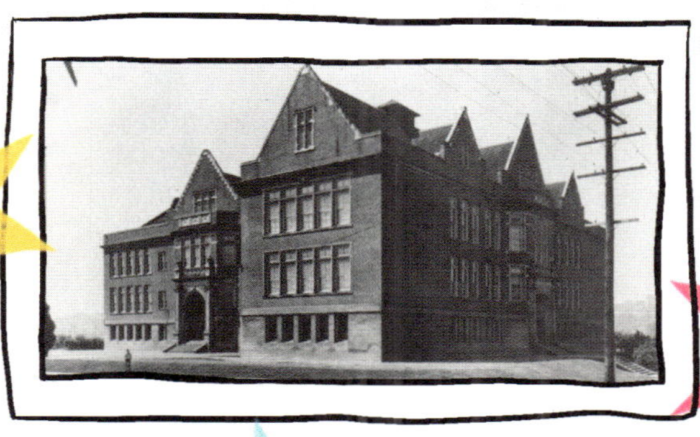

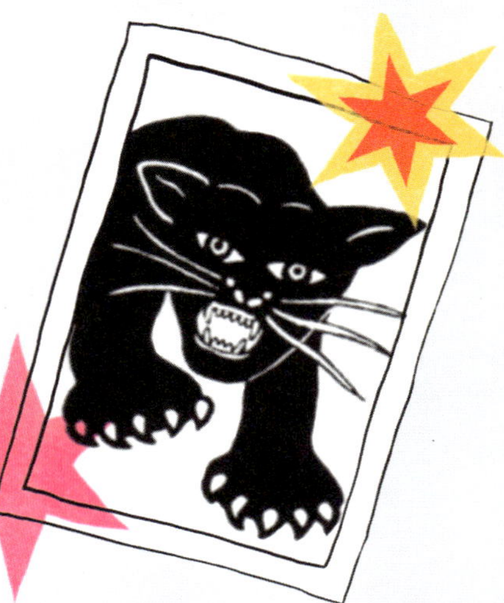

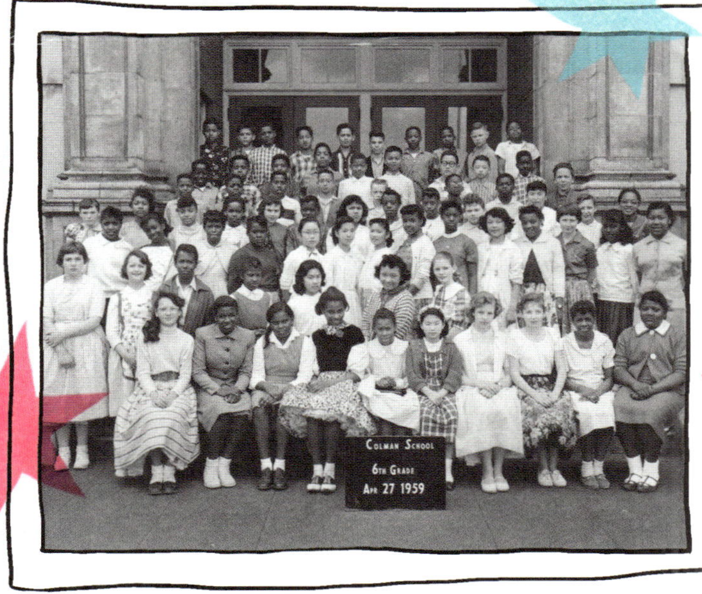
COLMAN SCHOOL
6TH GRADE
APR 27 1959

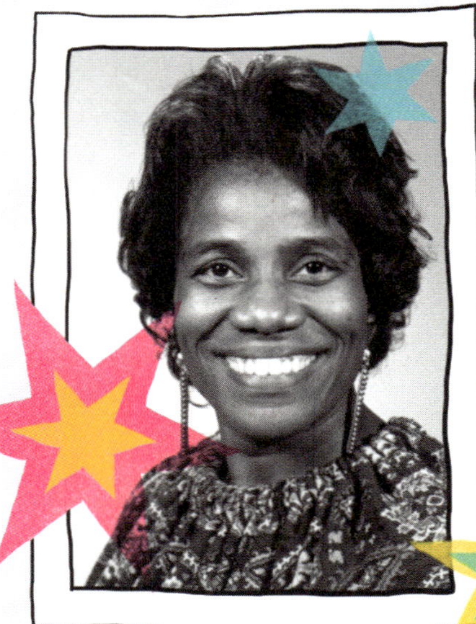

IN JUNIOR HIGH SCHOOL

we had to pick a book to read, and I picked the *Autobiography of Malcolm X* and was told that I could not read that book. So my father had to come down and deal with that, and he had read the book and didn't see why I couldn't read the book, and so I eventually got to read the book.

At Franklin High School, I was on the college track and actually could have graduated at sixteen. But Frank Hanawalt, the principal, said to my dad, "You know she's really bright, but you probably don't wanna put her in college right now."

I did have Josephine Funderburg, who is Black and a church member and a very good friend of my grandmother's and also a neighbor, who was my guidance counselor. I mean the reason why I was able to graduate at 16 was because of her. You had to have someone in your corner. If you didn't, you could easily just kind of fall through the cracks.

Leslie Womack

WHEN WE CAME BACK

from living in Mozambique, my family was renting out our house. So we moved in with my auntie Pat, who lived in Magnolia, and we all went to school in the north end, at Latona. I never had a Black ass elementary school experience. I was looking at a picture of my third grade class the other day. There were two Mexican kids and then a bunch of adopted kids from around the world adopted by whites in my class. We were the six people of color, but every parent was white except my parents.

I went to Meany for middle school, which to me was a real culture shock, because I do feel like I was so white-washed by the time I got to middle school. I ended up really learning the talent of code-switching and being able to be in different worlds.

I think I didn't understand how much racism played a role in every single thing I did until I was in my early twenties and started looking back and thinking, "Man, why didn't anybody make me a tutor in math?" I had a math class in highschool where I would finish all my work early. The teacher would have me help people in class, but I didn't get a title. She would have me make a Starbucks run for the class. Every day. Like the mindset was, "She's not going into AP math, she's done." No one ever said, "Let's do something better with her."

Eula Scott Bynoe

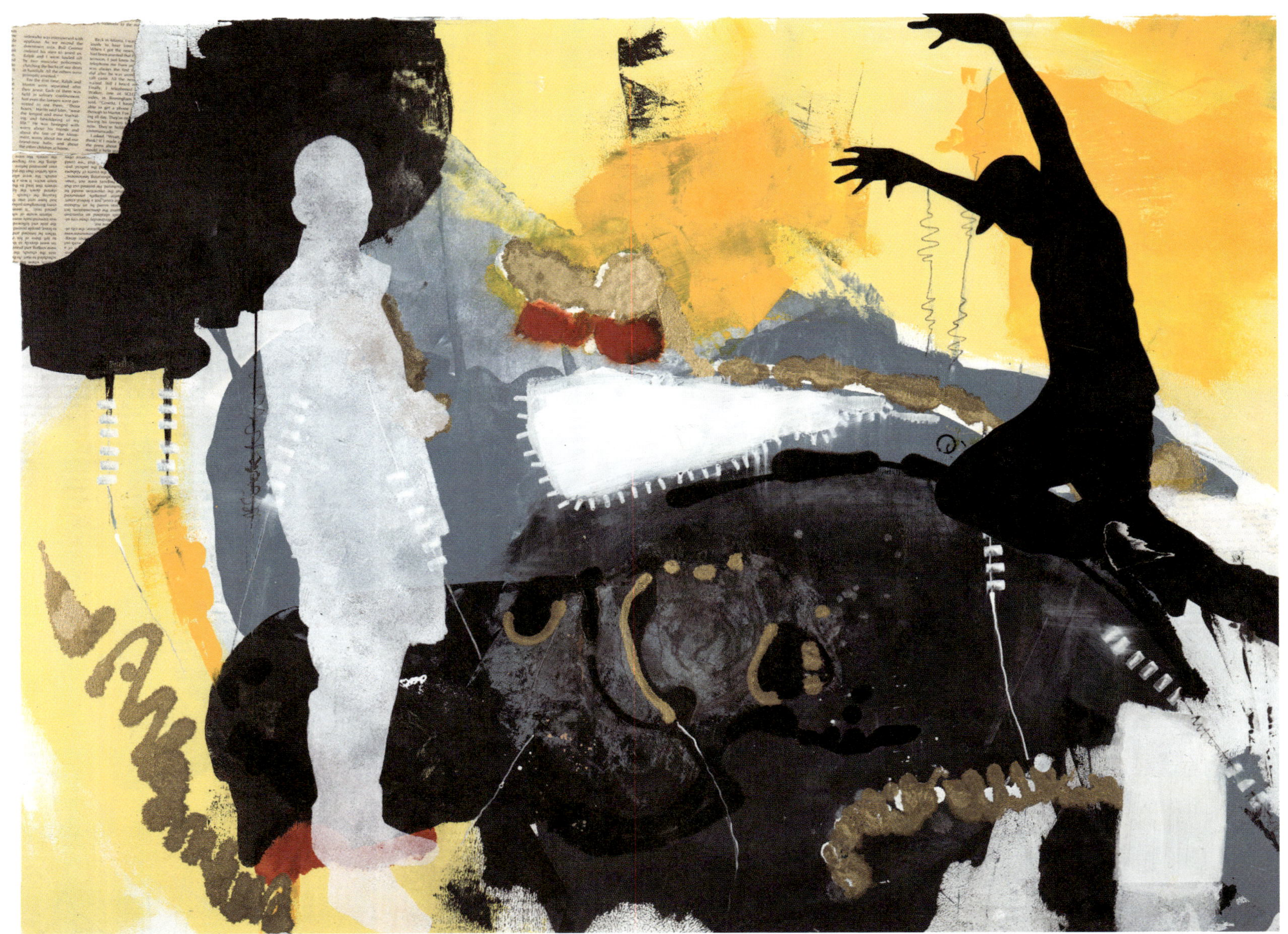

I CAN'T IMAGINE

what this city's arts community would look like without the Central District. Especially for young people, or people of color, who came through Langston at the time it thrived.

In the Parks Department, all of our programs for teens and pre-teens were free. It wasn't until the summer time that we had to charge for camps. Darcell Lorraine Hubbard introduced me to Langston and, at that time, the building was full, every day, of young people preparing for a performance of some kind. If they weren't preparing for a performance, they were there to watch somebody who was preparing for a performance. Steve Sneed, who was the director at the time, ran that facility along with Sheree Seretse, and the programs that they allowed young people to have in that building were unheard of. We did everything as a family.

The people I worked with, Charles Humphrey, Arthur Banks, Mark Smith, Steve Sneed, Reco Bembry, James King, they started the late-night program with the Parks Department. My sons call some of them uncle, you know. And my sons are thirty-four now. Ken Bounds, who was the superintendent of Parks and Recreation for a long time, came to me when my sons were trying to figure out what they were gonna do after high school. This is the superintendent. I'm a lowly rec attendant. He asks me what my sons are interested in and I say, "Well one wants to do what I'm doing, working with kids and performing, and the other one wants to be a pilot."

He said "I got a friend that owns a plane. He'll hook him up."

I blew it off. I'm like, "This guy doesn't know me."

The next day I receive an email from his friend and, that same day, he takes my son up in a plane.

The rest of that week my son is in a plane over Seattle.

My son chose to go to the Air Force based on the experience he got from my superintendent.

Isiah Anderson

BONNIE HOPPER
Untitled

MY NAME IS

Zola Mumford. I was born in Ruston, Louisiana, in 1968.

Both of my parents were part of the later great migration. My mother was from a small town, in northern Louisiana, and my dad was from Kentucky.

In my neighborhood, I attended Colman School and Leschi. I had some terrific teachers there. I could have walked to either Franklin or Garfield. But, the busing program came in. And I was assigned, for middle school, to go to Eckstein in the north end. It was incredibly polarized racially, racial slurs, people dead-set on sticking to their own group. I was kind of a nerd, so I hung out with multiracial nerds. We were a book family. I would be walking around with a collection of Ibsen plays and I'd have these white adults saying, "Do you understand that?"

Sometimes I would talk in class and mention a Black inventor or a Black person who had done something historically important, and that didn't go over well with some of my teachers.

At the time, it just felt like I was being piled on by every bully possible.
Sometimes the bullies were grownups. When I went to Leschi, during one of the periodic achievement assessment measuring test times, my scores were high even though I was already in the gifted program. This is the '70s, so you know, you're filling in the shaded bubbles on a form with a number two pencil. They took me into a separate room, some adults and a teacher, and they made me take the test again with folks watching me.

At the time I just thought, "Oh, maybe I didn't color these bubbles in dark enough like they said."

I went home and told my mom. She got on the phone.

I know that when I was on that bus, once we came back across that Montlake cut, I was like, okay, if something happens to me here, I know I can call for help, not just from immediate family, but from the extended community I had. I remember one time being on that bus, and a van pulled up alongside it. There were two young Black men driving it. And one of them pulled out this red, black and green flag and waved it at this kid. I mean, it's a bus full of Black kids getting bused. And he's holding this flag. And all the kids scream and start doing the Black power fist back. Those were some strange times. I think it was a terrible idea, the whole busing program. If anything, the experience cemented this sense I had that the Central District was where I could be creative and not be afraid...of everybody.

p112–113
ROMSON BUSTILLO
Central District

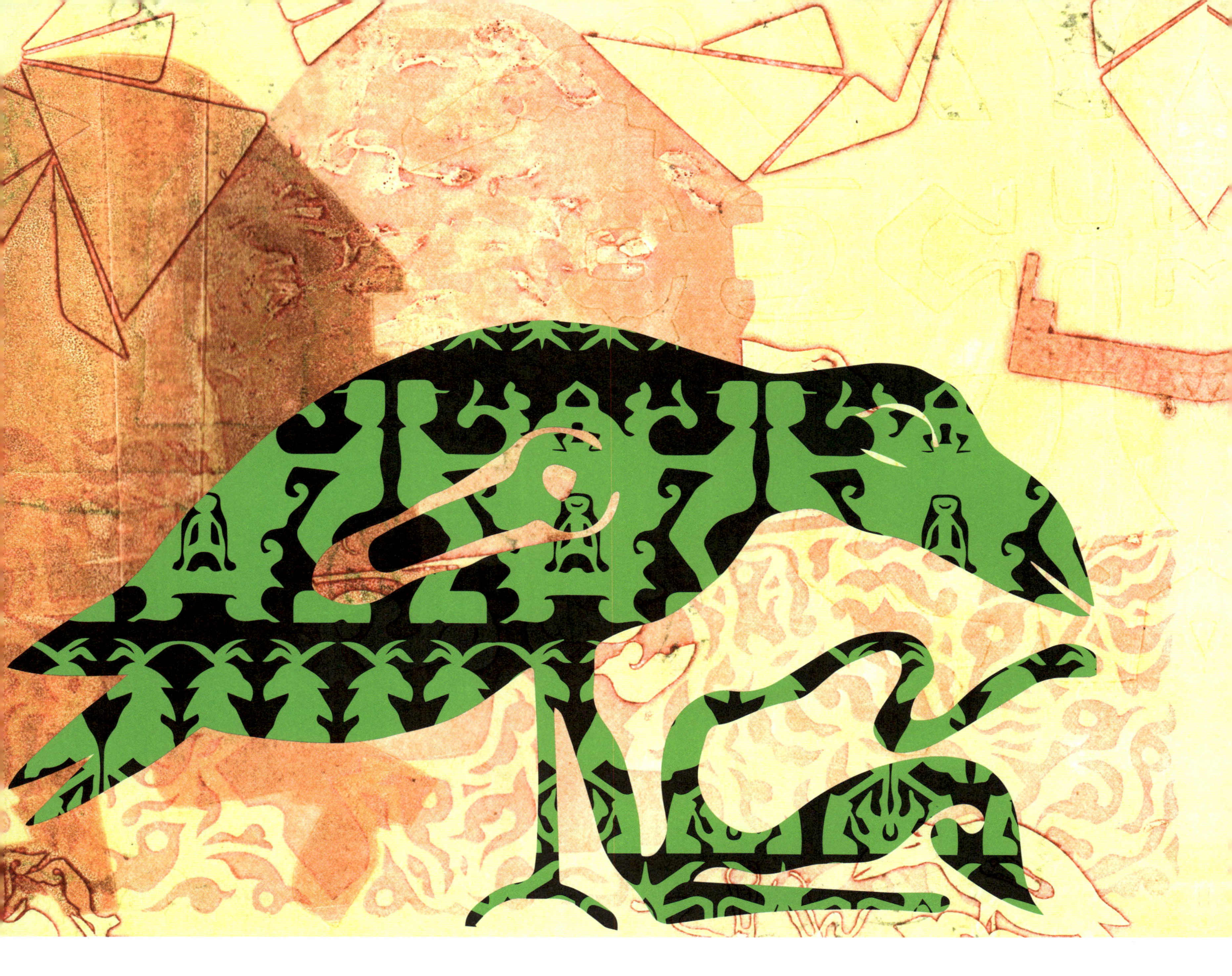

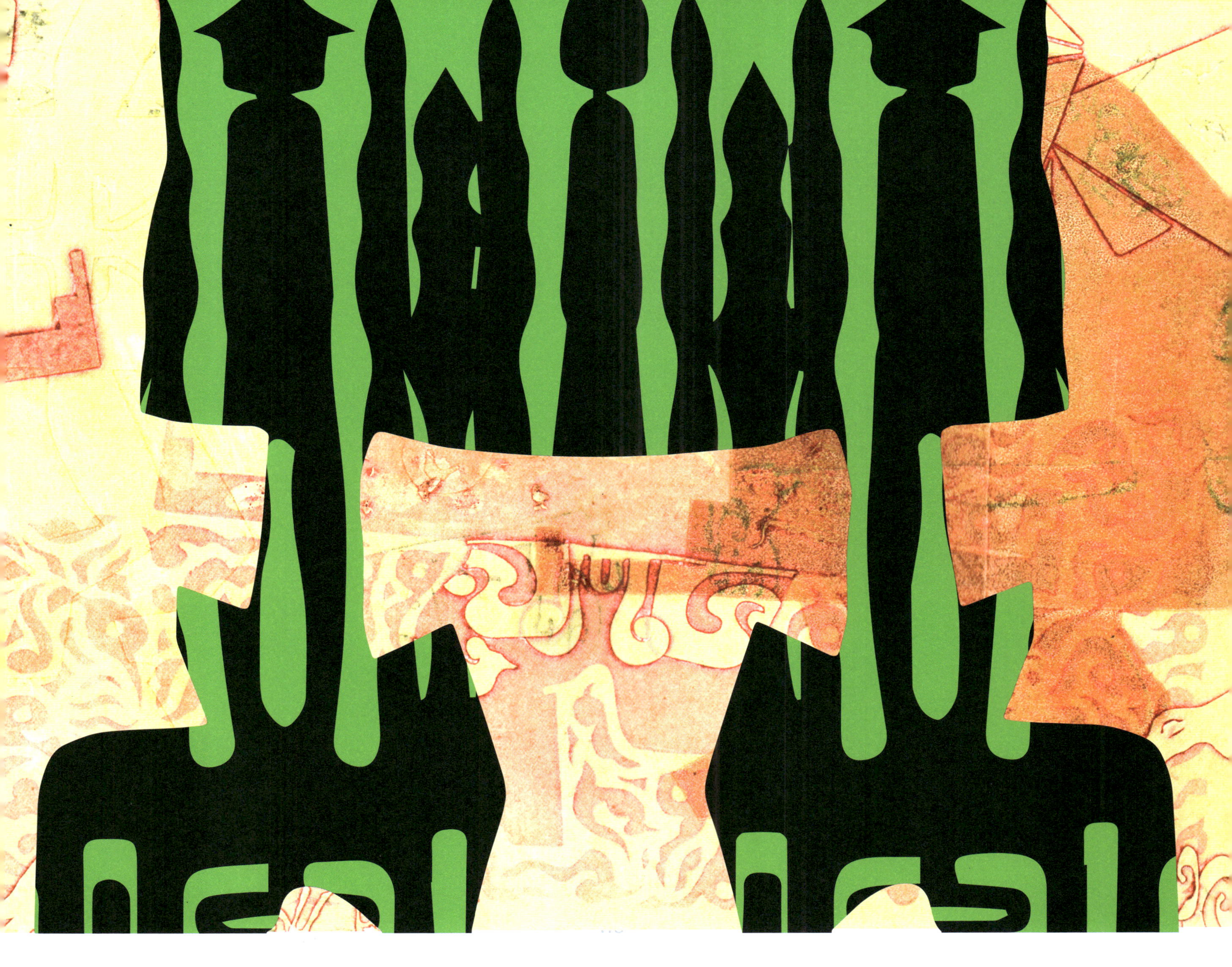

SIX

WORK

People that worked at Todd Shipyard, that
worked at Bethlehem Steel, worked for Boeing,
worked for Sears, could send their children into
a neighborhood store, and if you needed meat
or something, you signed credit, and they knew
who you were, and they knew that they were
going to get their money. It was actually a working community. Even when we were kids. Mr
Edwards was one of the most important people along with John Little, Charles Huey, Barry
Carter. Those were important people, because
they had jobs for us. When I was fourteen, fifteen years old, they didn't let me run the street.
They'd get me and say, "You workin', I got
something for you to do." Every summer I had
something to do.

Gary Hammon

I WAS FREELANCING

with an advertising agency, as a commercial artist. My neighbors couldn't figure out who I was. They knew I was working, I had a car, but they didn't understand why I was home all the time. They thought I was a cop. I had a Plymouth, looked like a cop car. And they thought, well, if he's not a cop, maybe he's a pimp. So, I told them, I'm an artist, I do commercial art. But they couldn't connect with that. So, little by little, I'd invite them up, and I'd show them the work I'm doing.

There was a lady, someone's grandmother, Black woman, across the street. She'd see me and "Hey, hey Mr. Doggett, are you going downtown?"

I'd give her a lift.

And she'd ask me, "Well, what do you do?"

And I told her, I do commercial art, and I do painting, and I exhibit. Went through the whole thing and explained it.

Then she says, "But what do you do?" She didn't see that as a job.

I started teaching art classes for kids and adults here, in my studio. The parents weren't sure about the kids going into art. They worried about the whole starving artist thing. They had no idea about the commercial arts. So, I had to talk to the parents and even to the teachers. Getting them to understand about letting the kids go if they want. Let them do it. Give them materials. Get them supplies.

Once in a while, I'm at a store somewhere, and a gentleman will come up to me, "Hey Al, Al Doggett. I used to take classes with you."

Al Doggett

DAMON BROWN
Al Doggett

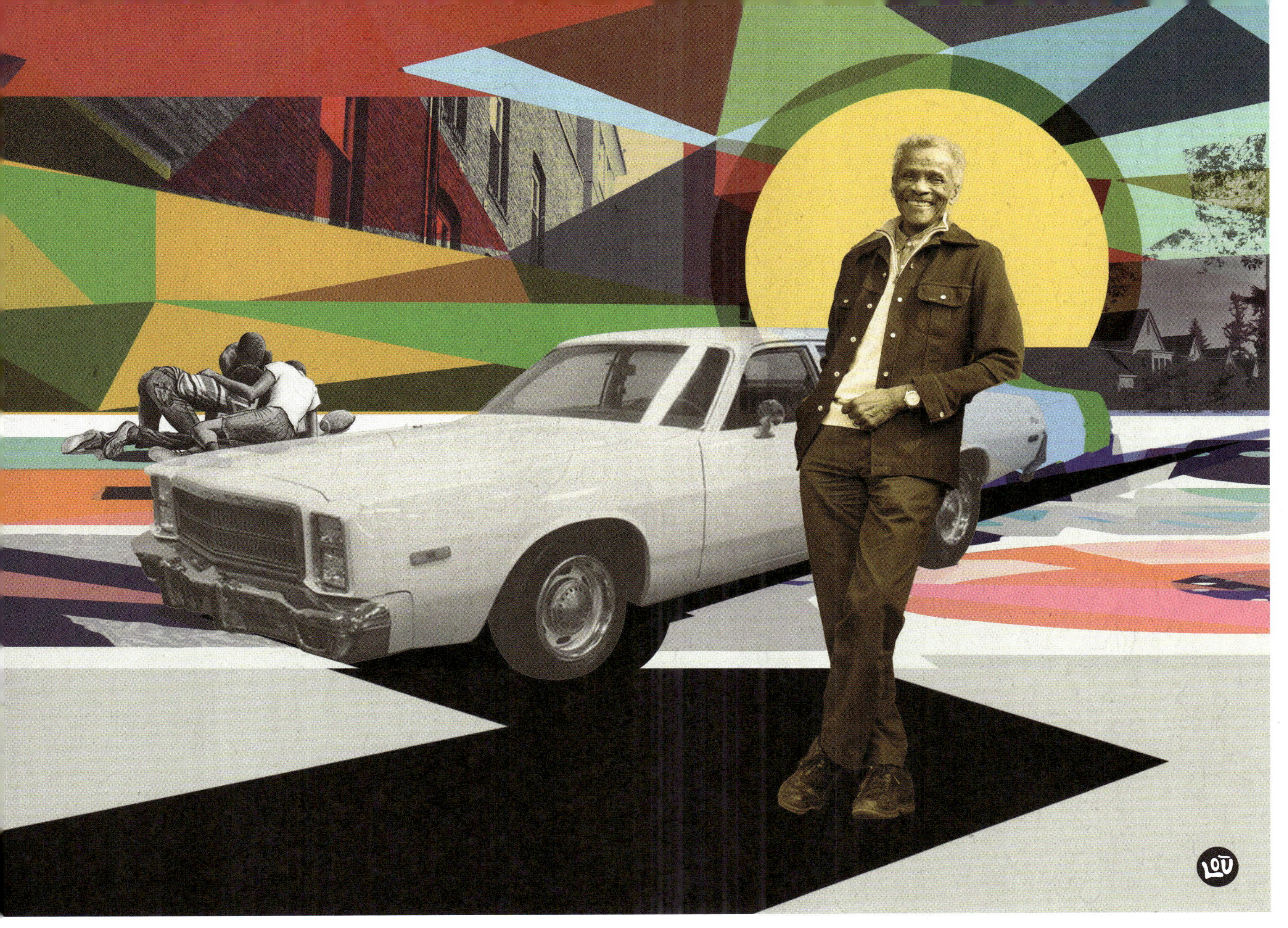

MY FATHER TOOK

several different jobs. He ended up at the post office.
And he was one of the first employees at Nordstrom.
He cleaned their stores. After that, he'd go to the
post office.

One day we were all eating dinner, that's when
you ate dinner together, and he looks down at
me and says,

"Boy, you eat too much. I need to put you to work."

So I joined the crew. I was eleven.

Of course my mother's like, "What's he gonna do?"

"Oh I'll find something for him to do."

So I cleaned the bathrooms and windows, picked up
paper and dumped the ashtrays at Nordstrom.

Gary Hammon

ONE OF
THE REASONS

the CD could be as good as it was is because people had stable jobs. If you didn't work at Boeing then you worked for the city or the school district. There was enough consistency in your life that you could feel like it was your community. I grew up with people who couldn't get a job anywhere else but the post office because they were Black. But they were still engaged in the community. I'm thinking of Rudolph Hill, who went to St. Clement's Church. He ran a Boy Scout troop, and a youth group at the church. He would come to every community meeting. You'd show up, there'd he'd be, organizing something. That kind of community building is hard to do when you have three jobs and you're constantly moving from one place to another.

Zola Mumford

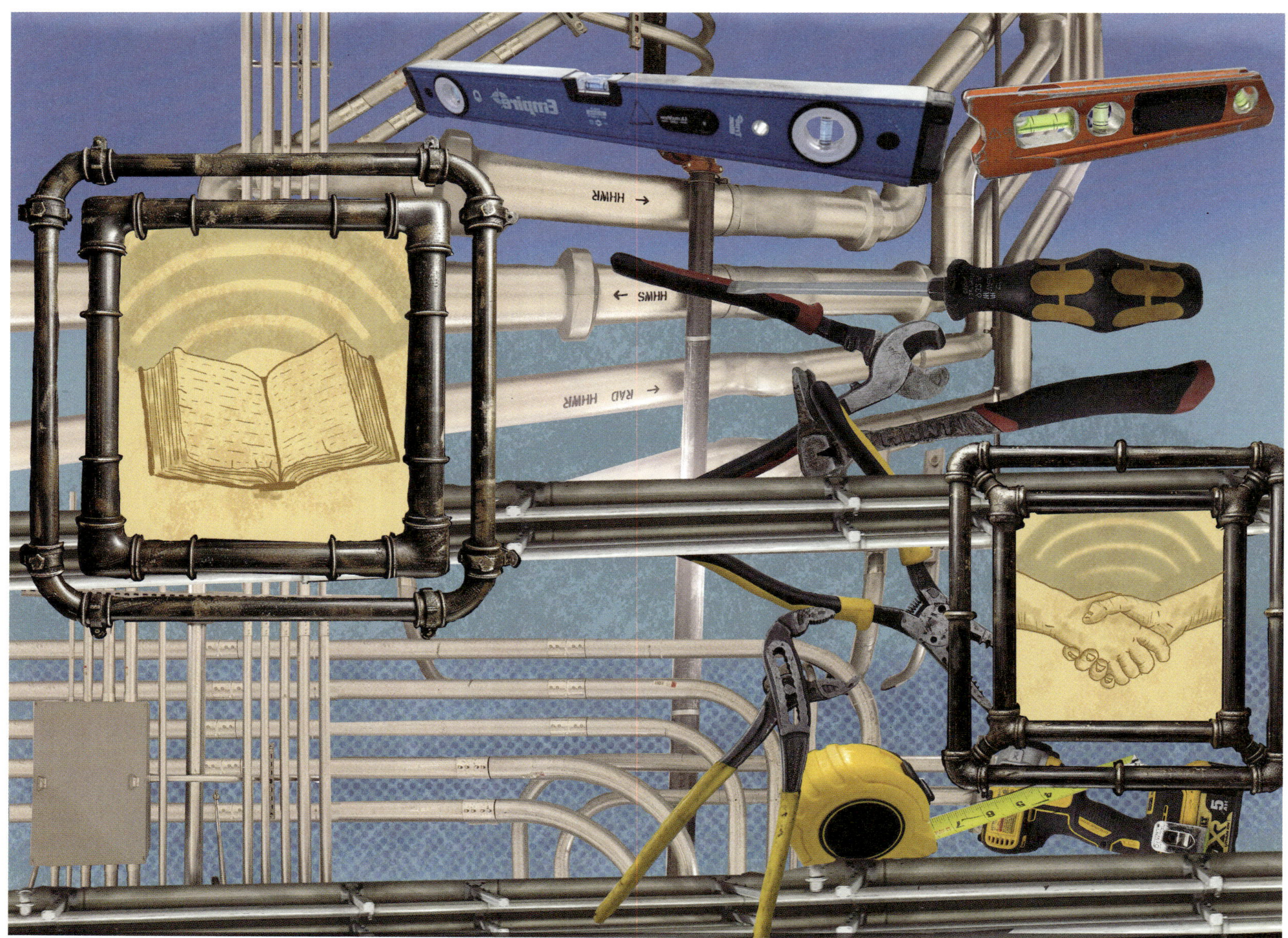

MY NAME IS

Gregory Scott. I grew up in South Central LA. My father's father was an electrical contractor here in Seattle, and when my dad joined him in his business, our family moved up here, to 17th and Yesler. I was seven.

In South Central Los Angeles, all I saw was Black people, and when we moved to 17th and Yesler, that used to be a Jewish and Asian neighborhood. My mother dropped me and my brother off, at an Asian barbershop. Customers kept coming in and coming in and coming in. My brother finally confronted the barber, and said, "We've been here. Why haven't we got our chance in the chair yet?" And he says, "Because I can't cut your hair."

My father, Tyree Scott, was a civil rights activist, and labor organizer, and I remember that we would get the tires on our cars cut, the windows knocked out. There were Molotov cocktail bombs found on the side of our house. My father went to jail often, and he was on TV about his fight to get people of color in the trade unions. That was a good time in my life, you know, seeing Black people stand up for themselves.

CHI MOSCOU-JACKSON
Untitled

And my father taught me to stand up for myself. When I was seventeen years old, I got a summer job at a construction site. I was working on a highway site, where they would dig really big holes in the ground and put those things in that are called vaults, for the sewage to go through. It was a union job. The supervisor came over to me and said, "We need two men and a boy on that pipe." Obviously, I was the boy, because the other two people were white men, so I came home and I told my father, and he said, "What did you do about it?" And I said, "Nothing." So he gave me this list of things to go back and tell that employer the next day. I carry that with me every time I'm on a job site. If I'm ever confronted, or if I feel that I'm being misused, I confront the situation there.

The way I got that job was I just walked onto the site. The guy asked me, "Are you from the union?" and I said, "Yeah." I worked about four days, and he came over and he said, "Hey, man, you're not in the union. You can't be on this job unless you're in the union. Go join tomorrow." So, when I was 17 years old, I got my first book, and I've been involved in a lot of trade unions since then. I've been a pipe fitter at Todd Shipyard, I've been a plastic bench mechanic at Boeing. I've always been proud to be a union man. I'll stand up for the union in a heartbeat. I'm fifty-eight years old and I've never crossed a picket line. Extremely proud to say that.

Gregory Scott

I ENDED UP GOING TO

Seattle Central. Back then, Broadway was such a big deal. The movies were up there, you could go kick it at the Broadway Market. There was always somewhere to eat, really good, interesting, and different food. I knew I wanted to be a chef long before any of this, so food was always such a big deal to me.

When I finished up the culinary program at Seattle Central, I moved to the Central District. I was on 26th and Madison. I worked for Nordstrom for a while and learned a lot of customer service, a lot of professionalism, that was really important. I went from there and worked at Plenty. Jim Watkins was a Black chef. It was a deli, wine store and, at night, it was a restaurant, on 32nd and Union, in Madrona. That was pretty instrumental in my development as a chef. I went from there to KingFish, and started cooking lunch there. I learned a lot because that was my first time being on the line. Tracy McRay was my chef, and she was a hard ass. She was excellent and she wanted to make sure you were too. Man, I worked. I learned about work ethic, and then I just learned a lot about food, and where it came from, and treating it with respect, and learning how to cooperatively work with vendors. It was a really good experience for me. It really kind of set the tone for where I am at right now, because I was able to take what they gave me and then add my own thing.

Kristi Brown

KEN'S GAS STATION

Owned by Kenny Fukitami. 1625 East Yesler. Kenny was the first job I ever got. I was sixteen years old. It was during the gas crunch of 1973. He had his regular customers, not just Asian people, but Black people and white people as well, that were his regulars. Some of those people would buy gas on credit and pay him at the end of the month.

The gas lines would go four, five, six blocks back. Around the corner.

Kenny would say, "OK Daryl, it's almost five o'clock. You know what you gotta do."

I was the scapegoat. I had a sign, and I had to count ten cars back and pin that to the back of the last car that was gonna get gas that day. Sorry, this is it. And they would freak out. Because sometimes they'd be sitting there for forty-five minutes to an hour waiting on gas. And here comes this young kid with a sign.

Daryl Lockhart

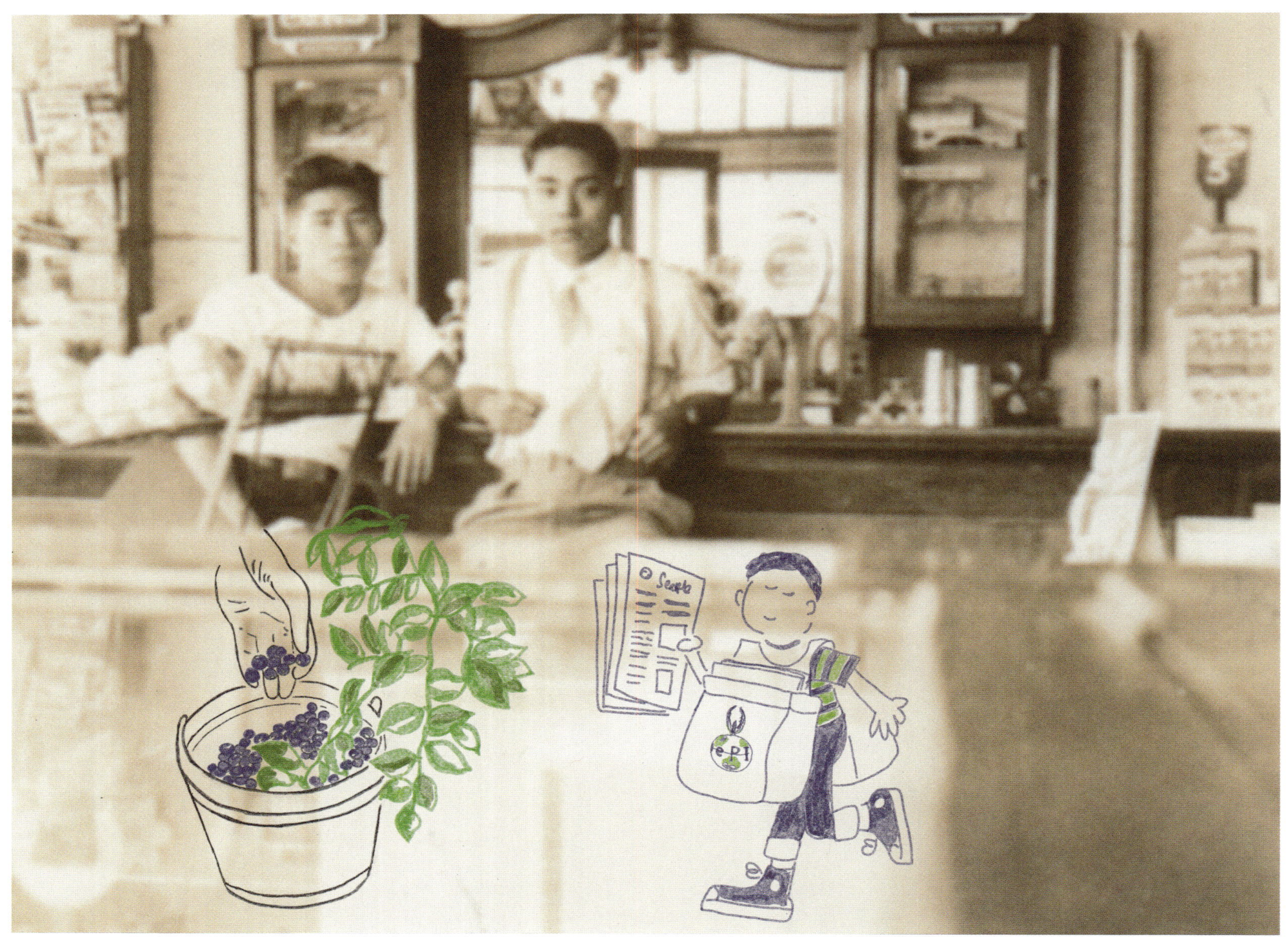
Scoop
ePI

MOST JAPANESE KIDS,

during the summers, we would go down into the Kent Valley. That place used to be just covered with nothing but farms. There were a lot of Japanese farms there, owned free and clear by Japanese farmers. We'd all go there to work and pick crops in the summertime.

Denny Tanaka would come in and drive around the CD and pick up all these kids that were going to go pick crops for them. We'd all go out in the fields for six or eight hours and come back home in the evening.

I think the first time I started would have been when I was in Washington Junior High School. About the seventh grade maybe. Before that, I worked at Tokuda

Drug Store up there at 18th and Yesler. I used to deliver prescriptions around the neighborhood. George Tokuda used to take me fishing along with his son Kippy, Kip Tokuda. He was almost like, I wouldn't say a second daddy, but he was a nice guy.

But I first started working when I was ten. I would get up at about 4:00am and go deliver PI newspapers around the neighborhood. It was a big route. It went from Day Street and 29th Avenue, by the African American Museum, down to 27th Avenue and as far north as Main Street. That was a huge area. That was all in the dark. I thought it was great. Everybody else I knew thought I was really stupid, a ten-year old kid delivering papers in

ERIN SHIGAKI
Tagawa—Work

the dark before school. But there weren't that
many people in the Japanese community that
were as poor as us either.

I especially enjoyed learning the paper route
from this Black brother. He was an old guy,
one whole grade ahead of us. It was cool being
able to hang out with him. The only thing that
was bad about delivering papers was the collection part. I'd go out there to collect for the
paper, and I would get no answer at all. I was
never able to collect from this one house. When
I'd knock on the door sometimes I would get
this, "My mama's not home right now. You got
to come back later." But like an adult trying to
talk in a kid voice so they wouldn't have to pay
for their paper. That was the only negative part
of the whole thing, getting stiffed by people. I
was like, "Man I got to pay for these papers."
But I liked getting up early and getting out
there doing something.

Mike Tagawa

MY NAME IS

DeCharlene Williams. I was born in 1943, in a little town called Temple, Texas.

I ended up in Seattle because I married when I was fifteen. I went over to Edison Technical School and I finished before I was sixteen and a half. Then I took a test out at Boeing and I made it. I went in there for employment. I looked at the fellows there. They was all looking at me grinning and everything. I said, "I've got to get out of here." Because I was a Black woman and they was all white men. You could tell what they wanted to do. They thought they was going to feel and touch me. I wouldn't allow that. I quit that job.

I called my mother and she said, "Go on down there to the beauty college. You wanted to be a beautician, go there and learn."

So I went over here to Everette's Beauty School. I was about seventeen and a half when I finished. I took the state board and passed it on my first time. I worked for a lady named Alberta Woodard, right up in the Mount Baker district. They liked to play the horse races in there.

They had bookies that come in there taking out bets on the race.

I didn't like that, so I went to Virgie's salon down the hill on 28th and Madison. Got in there and it was the worst shop I ever been in in my life. She was a gambler. She chased young men. She was playing the horses, the dogs. The landlord booted her out because she wouldn't pay her rent, so she moved up the hill and I went with her. At that place, she didn't pay the bills. The public utilities came in and cut off our lights while I was doing a lady with a permanent. I had to go next door and rinse the perm out of the lady's hair.

I said, "I got to get around and find me something."

I found out Virgie's building was for sale. I said to Virgie, "Are you interested in buying it?"

"No, I'm not interested in buying it. They not going to sell it to you. You a woman and they don't sell to women."

I went to thirty banks and none of them would loan me the money. I went into Metropolitan Federal Saving and Loan downtown. I put in a notebook how much I was going to pay them. I wanted a thirty-year loan. The lady says, "All this looks fine and good but there's only one thing. You're a woman and they ain't going to okay no loan for no woman because they don't let women buy commercial property, only men."

I said, "Just take this and put my check on here; it's $6500. Take it back there to your manager, and see what he has to say about it."

She took it and went back there. She came out and she said, "Oh, he went for it!"

The day I moved in was April 4th. They had just killed Martin Luther King. I had a beautiful glass table. They told me Martin Luther King had been shot dead, assassinated. I bloomphed (*pantomimes falling over*), broke my table, I cried like a baby. I was crying for Martin Luther King and I was crying for my beautiful table I had just broke. Been in there ever since. I been there for forty-eight years.

My shop has meant everything to my customers, because we're like family. A lady, not so long ago, told her daughter, had it written up in her will, she wanted me to go buy her dress, and do her hair, when she died, everything from DeCharlene. "Nobody else but DeCharlene. Let her dress me. I want to go out with the DeCharlene look."

I have customers that have moved out to Federal Way and Kent, and they still come. They live out there because the rent is cheap and they have no place else to go. A lot of them are on fixed incomes. This is why I have a senior day. My senior day is Tuesday and Wednesday and that accommodates people on fixed income. My dream has been to make all women beautiful. That's my dream.

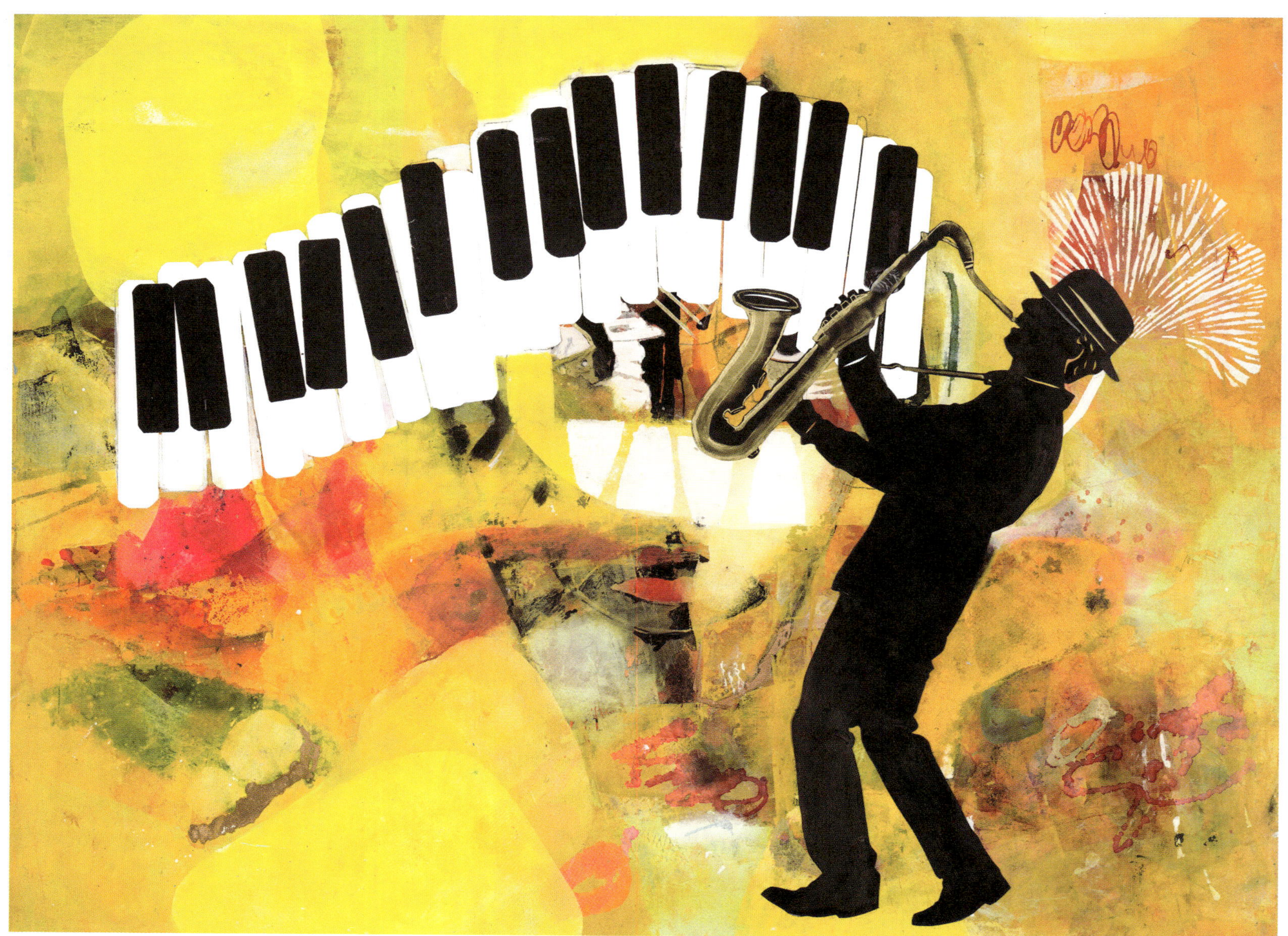

MY NAME IS

Leslie Webb Womack. I was born in Seattle, Washington, in 1957.

When my grandparents moved here, it was very common that, as more people would migrate here, they would stay with whoever was already here, until they got on their feet. My family came here during the 40s. My paternal grandmother worked in the naval shipyards, which was common, there were jobs.

When I was born, my mom went back to work at Boeing, and I stayed with my grandparents all the time, in the Central Area. It was a vibrant, close-knit place that fully provided everything for us. You know, the grocery store, our dentist, our doctors, our dry cleaning, our records, our entertainment was all right here. So, even though we were redlined into this area, we still managed to provide and get all of the things we needed here.

My grandmother on my mother's side, she was an entrepreneur. She owned a dry cleaners and eventually owned a record store on Madison Street. It was called The Little Record Mart. She actually purchased it, and I started working for her when I was seven, so I say that I've worked all my life.

I sold records. She kind of specialized in jazz, and we would go to the wholesale house and pick out the latest jazz records, and then we would sell them. She featured penny candy, that was her thing that would bring people in, and then she would have things playing, and they would end up buying a ninety-nine cent 45, but she had a huge album collection as well.

There was a pool hall across the street, there was a beauty shop next to that, and those were all long-standing businesses where, if you needed change for a twenty, you went across the street to the beauty shop.

I could never, ever go into the pool hall. But I remember my grandmother needed change one day, and the beauty shop was closed, and she goes, "Okay, I'm sending you in there and I'm expecting you back in five minutes." I mean these guys were in there drinking and playing pool. It's dark, it's smoky. Everyone's calling you, "Hey, baby." But they're not doin' anything, because they know you're Ms. Gibbon's granddaughter. They wouldn't dare, you know?

One of the reasons my grandmother was an entrepreneur was that she didn't want, she goes, "I don't want white people tellin' me what to do. And the only way that's gonna happen is for me to have my own business."

I DID GET A VAST ARRAY

of jobs when I got here. I was a busboy at a Sizzler, I did landscaping, I performed every-where, and then I got connected with the Yesler Community Center, with a young lady by the name of Darcell Lorraine. She was somebody who grew up here, and her family lived across the street from Langston Hughes, so she was into theater and performing, and lip syncing at the time was huge.

So I started volunteering at the Yesler Community Center, teaching a group of kids how to lip sync. It was a group called the MoTown Review. And we had kids aging from five to seventeen doing Michael Jackson, the Jackson Five, Temptations, you name it. They would tour. Darcelle got me connected with that as a volunteer. But then they offered me a job.

I've been with the Parks Department ever since, twenty-eight years now, and I never inter-viewed with the City of Seattle. They just, "You want the job?"

"Sure!"

"Fill out this paperwork. There you go."

At that time, I thought, "If you don't have a job in Seattle you're not looking to work." Too many jobs. I guess I was coming from a place where there were no jobs. We had college edu-cated individuals applying for janitorial jobs in Chicago. Here it was just too easy. And I took advantage of it.

I was a dancer, a choreographer, stand up comedian, and MC.

I always said, "I'm only working at the city until I get my big break." Five years went by and "I'm just here until I get my big break!" And then ten years went by, and my son's still growing, and "I'm only here until I get my big break." And fifteen years go by, and then I'm like, "You know, this is my job. This is where I'll be until my son gets his big break."

Isiah Anderson

ROMSON BUSTILLO
Isiah

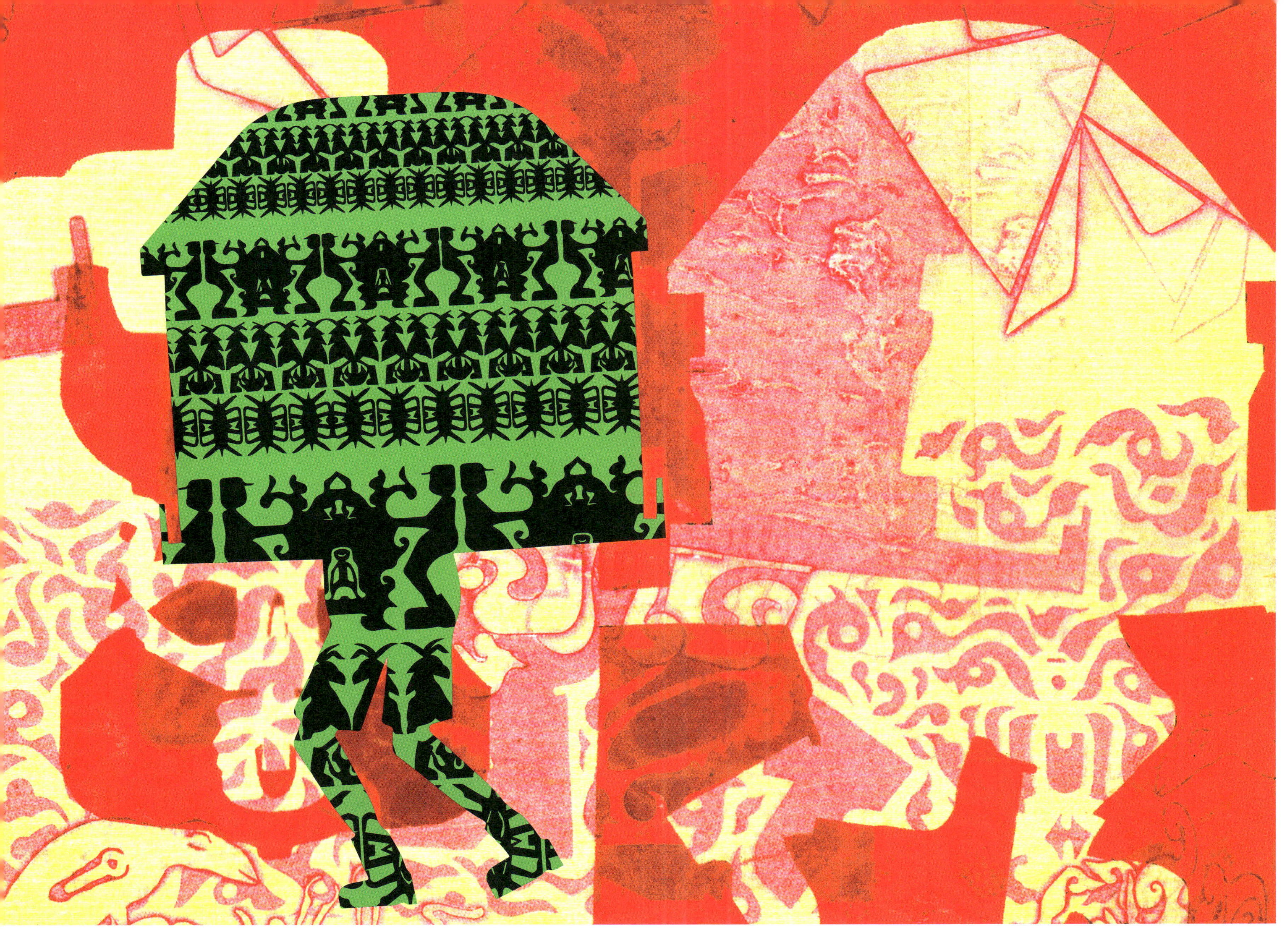

WE HAD A LAUNDROMAT

and dry cleaning place up on 23rd and Spring, Sunshine Center. It got too much for us, after a while, seven days a week. So we went to Boeing. When we both got laid off, he went to King County Metro, driving a bus.

He said, "Why don't you try for customer service at King County Metro?"

I did and that's where I retired, thirty-one years later. I went from on-call operator, to manager, to supervisor of customer service. At that time we had books, big old books, with all the bus routes in there. I knew those books inside out. I could sit up and knit and crochet when I was on the phones. When somebody told me where they were and where they were going, I could just give them the route information they needed.

I didn't ever think that we would go to computer. Paul Tolliver came down with this little floppy disk and there was a computer sitting on my supervisor's desk, and he said, "You know what, Lottie? Eventually I'm gonna give you this floppy disk and you gonna have to bring up whatever I need on here," and I thought "Oh God, I'll never do that." I would never do that. It was so scary.

They told me, "When people call in, you gonna have to put in the computer where they're leaving from and where they're going to, and then the computer will give them the information on how to get there."

And I thought, "That ain't never gonna work." But it did, of course it did.

Then it came to a point that we couldn't live without it. When the system went down, you know, everything went down.

I loved that job. I loved customer service, I love people. I ain't never thought about myself getting no award, but I received the Martin Luther King award for King County! That was a celebration, we had it at the Benaroya Hall, and they invited everybody. My church came, my neighbors came, all these committees I was on came. I thought, "Now, you know, this is awesome."

Lottie Cross

SEVEN

RESISTANCE & COLLECTIVE POWER

I'm pretty sure it was Inye Wokoma who first
shared with me the idea that the city of Seattle
was shaped by what happened in the Central
District. The people who were redlined into the
CD had to create their own solutions in ways that
other neighborhoods did not, and the result-
ing processes of creativity, innovation, self-determination, interdependence, and resistance
reverberated out into the rest of the city, shaping
policy and culture.

I think the stories in this chapter offer some of
the best examples of that. Whether it was the
Black Panthers showing the city what mutual
aid looks like, through breakfast programs and
community clinics; or Black tradespeople shut-
ting down construction projects to desegregate
the unions; or stealthy interventions that revealed
housing discrimination at every level of the private and public sector; the entire city matured and
took shape in the bright light of that change.

Jill Freidberg

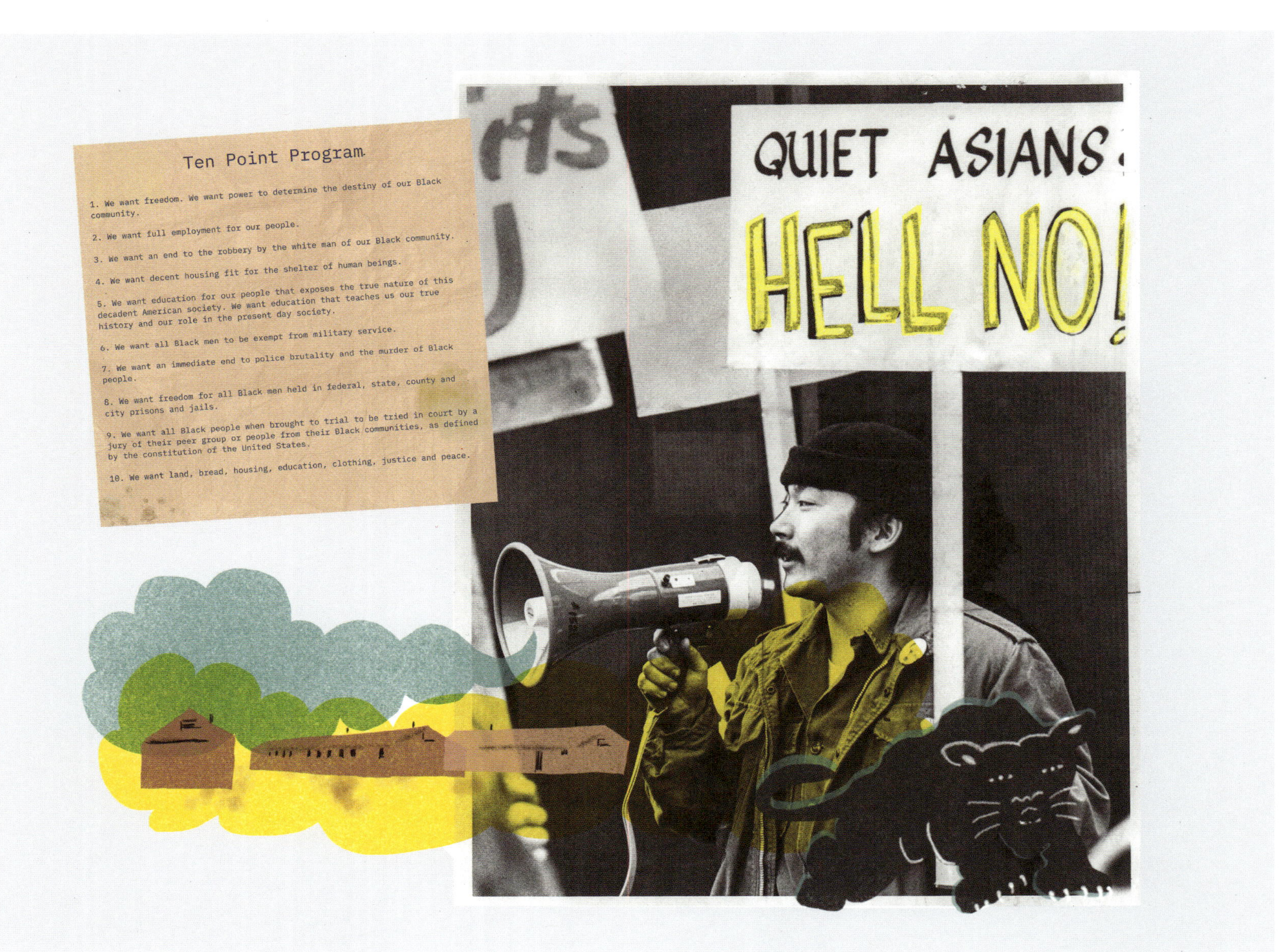

Ten Point Program

1. We want freedom. We want power to determine the destiny of our Black community.

2. We want full employment for our people.

3. We want an end to the robbery by the white man of our Black community.

4. We want decent housing fit for the shelter of human beings.

5. We want education for our people that exposes the true nature of this decadent American society. We want education that teaches us our true history and our role in the present day society.

6. We want all Black men to be exempt from military service.

7. We want an immediate end to police brutality and the murder of Black people.

8. We want freedom for all Black men held in federal, state, county and city prisons and jails.

9. We want all Black people when brought to trial to be tried in court by a jury of their peer group or people from their Black communities, as defined by the constitution of the United States.

10. We want land, bread, housing, education, clothing, justice and peace.

MY NAME IS

Michael Tagawa. I was born in 1944, in the Minidoka concentration camp, in southern Idaho.

Daddy died in 1952, seven years after we got out of the camps. I never really got to know him because, for the last couple years of his life, he was in Firland Sanitarium which is that tubercular place up there on about 175th and 15th. That's where my grandfather was too. They both ended up dying there.

After that, it was all left up to my mom to be the breadwinner. She had five of us kids and her mother and father. It was pretty tough on her.

My first wife Judy and I were in the Arboretum the first time we saw the Black Panthers marching around. Bobby White, who I first met in fifth grade, came up and told me that I had to join the Party right now.

I said, "Hey Bobby, look here man, I ain't Black."

He said "You ain't white either."

ERIN SHIGAKI
Tagawa—Activism

Judy, right from the get-go, was like "You got to join." That was in the early days of the Party; summer of '68. Judy taught me a lot. She taught me not to be so damn impulsive, which might have actually saved my ass in a couple of instances. There were a lot of days when things were going on that she knew about but wasn't a part of; activities that occurred in the CD that might have been a lot worse if she wasn't there saying, "You can be as committed and intense as you want, but don't be stupid." That's basically what her message was. Her being just a little bit outside of the Party, she was able to say, "That's a dumb ass idea. You do that, you're going to get yourself killed." She was just a good, level-headed, kind-hearted, white person who had a big influence on me.

Me, Garry Owens, who I met when I was a kid living at Rainier Vista housing projects, Bobby White, Bobby Harding...we were all the old guys. We all graduated from Garfield or Franklin in 1962. Then it was strange how we all independently came together, at the age of twenty-four, right after the Black Panther Party started, to join up with these teenagers. We'd all been through the military and come back to Seattle, and now Civil Rights were on fire. We all decided that we're going to join this thing called the Black Panther Party that was started here by these teenagers. Here we were mature, worldly veterans joining up with these young teenage radicals talking about fighting with guns. At that time it seemed to make sense to us.

For the most part, being in the Party meant just being out in the community and being visible. Some of us probably didn't have a good appreciation for non-violent protests, although we all do now. At the time we thought that the only way to do it was to get yourself a piece and get out there with the Party and patrol the neighborhood that you live in and follow the police around just to see if they stop somebody. If they stop somebody, you're supposed to get out of your car and stand there with your hardware hanging off you, your rifle, shotguns, pistols, whatever. Make it plain to whoever's been stopped that we're there watching the whole thing.

One time we went down to Rainier Beach because the kids were getting messed with by the whites. We chased a principal out of Rainier Beach. That moment gave a lot of people in the Central District a clearer idea about the Party. Then we had another confrontation at Bluma's Delicatessen, up on 25th and Cherry. It used to be where all the Garfield kids would hang out in the latter years of the '60s. But it evolved into being a place where kids would go and get drugs. They were openly dealing shit. Until the Panthers shut them down.

In the early days, we didn't get much support from anybody. But one family I can mention, because everybody knows them, is the Kurose family. They supported the Party. There were other Japanese families that came around to Party headquarters. It was kind of on the sly, a private thing. They wanted to donate money and help the Black Panther Party, which I always kind of thought was interesting too, because the Japanese are always considered to be so law-abiding and non-confrontational. They weren't being confrontational, but they were definitely supporting probably the most confrontational group in the whole city, which was pretty cool.

WE DID MARCH

I remember that, and I remember my mother had dyed my white shoes red, and it was pouring down rain, and the dye was coming off! I think my parents thought the Panthers were kind of militant, but one of the great things was the breakfast program. I think everybody, young and old, rallied around that.

Leslie Womack

WHAT A LOT OF PEOPLE DON'T KNOW

is that the first Head Start program for kids, in the United States, was right here in Seattle, and I was the Transportation Director of that program. I'd make out the routes and send buses out to pick kids up, to take them to a different school. We picked up kids all over Seattle. Then another program was called Mini Transit. We had fifteen passenger buses that went all through the Central Area, to people's homes. They could get on the bus for a dime, ride downtown, do their business in the county, city buildings, pay their taxes whatever, get on the bus and come back home. And then we had buses that picked up senior citizens and took them to hospitals or to go shopping. You see those buses now called Metro Access? That came from the Mini Transit program.

Cecil Beatty

I REMEMBER THE RIOTS

that kind of broke out. My mom said, "You're not going anywhere." She was like, "Sit down." But then when I got to Seattle Central Community College, we were forming a Black Student Union. Larry Gossett was one of the people that helped form the Black Student Union, and we walked out of school one day in protest of the dean. We chained the doors. We could see these big, black cars and flashbulbs going off, and I asked, "Is that the news people?" And someone said, "No, honey, that's the FBI. You're gonna have a file with them."

Vicky Garner

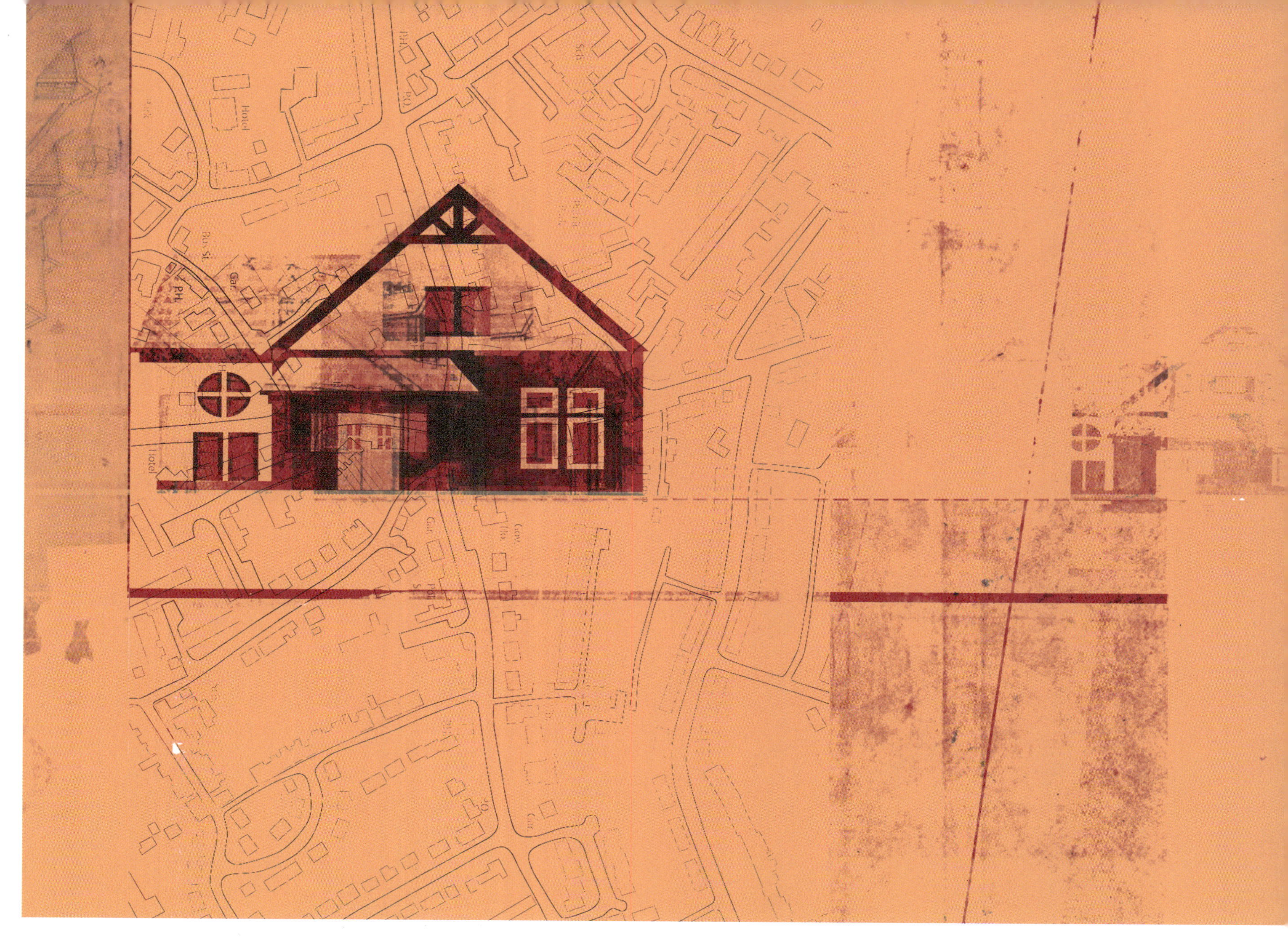

MY NAME IS

Joan Singler. Born in a suburb of Detroit called East Detroit. I went to Wayne State University and was about to embark on a career as a flight attendant for Pan Am, but I wanted to get some proficiency in Spanish, so I got a job working for the Teamsters in Detroit. That's where I met Ed, who was also working for the Teamsters. That plan to fly for Pan Am went out the window.

I'm Ed Singler. I was born in Detroit. My dad was a union leader. My mother worked for a union.

Joan: Ed was drafted and sent out to Seattle. We lived above Berg's Marina on Lake Union.

In 1961, I was pregnant with our first child. Ed and I went to see a production of *Raisin in the Sun*. Afterwards we started talking about the play with some other students, and we started talking about Seattle, and we decided to have another meeting.

Ed: Seattle at that time was a very segregated city. There were no Black people in any key jobs like police or fire, anything like that. So we said we gotta do something, we can't just sit here and let this kinda stuff go on.

Joan: There were so many meetings. And, a lot of phone calls.

Ed: And a lot of walking. We had to hand deliver those flyers and leaflets to the Central Area.

Joan: We were just trying to introduce our-selves. That we're part of Congress of Racial Equality, a national organization, and we're trying to do something about discrimination in housing and jobs and schools. We had the first picket at Safeway, on October 28th, two days before I delivered on October 30th! This was on Pine, just off of 23rd. They wouldn't hire Black workers.

The FBI was on us just like that. One of the CORE members was Norm Johnson, and he went to Mount Zion church. The FBI went to Reverend McKinney and told him, "You better check on one of your parishioners here because he's in big trouble. He's hooked up with a bunch of communists."

Tim Martin, who was chair of CORE for awhile, and his wife Georgia, had four kids and they searched and searched for a house to buy. Georgia's white, and every time she called, they'd have a house to show, and then they would ask her about her phone number, because the prefix was "East," EA. And if you gave that number, the realtors became very suspicious of who was actually calling. Every time they found a place, and the neighbors found out about it, they would raise holy hell, and the seller would back out. Tim finally found a place on the east-side where he had to deliver the earnest money, at night, in cash, so the neighbors wouldn't see.

So we put together "Operation Window Shop," where we'd bring Black people who were look-ing for homes to real estate offices outside of the Central District. They'd ask to see a home. They'd be denied. Then we'd send in a white couple to ask about the same home.

Ed: When we announced "Operation Window Shop," when we announced that we were going to send people out to real estate offices, all the real estate offices in King County decided to close. On a Sunday. You couldn't have bought a house if you tried.

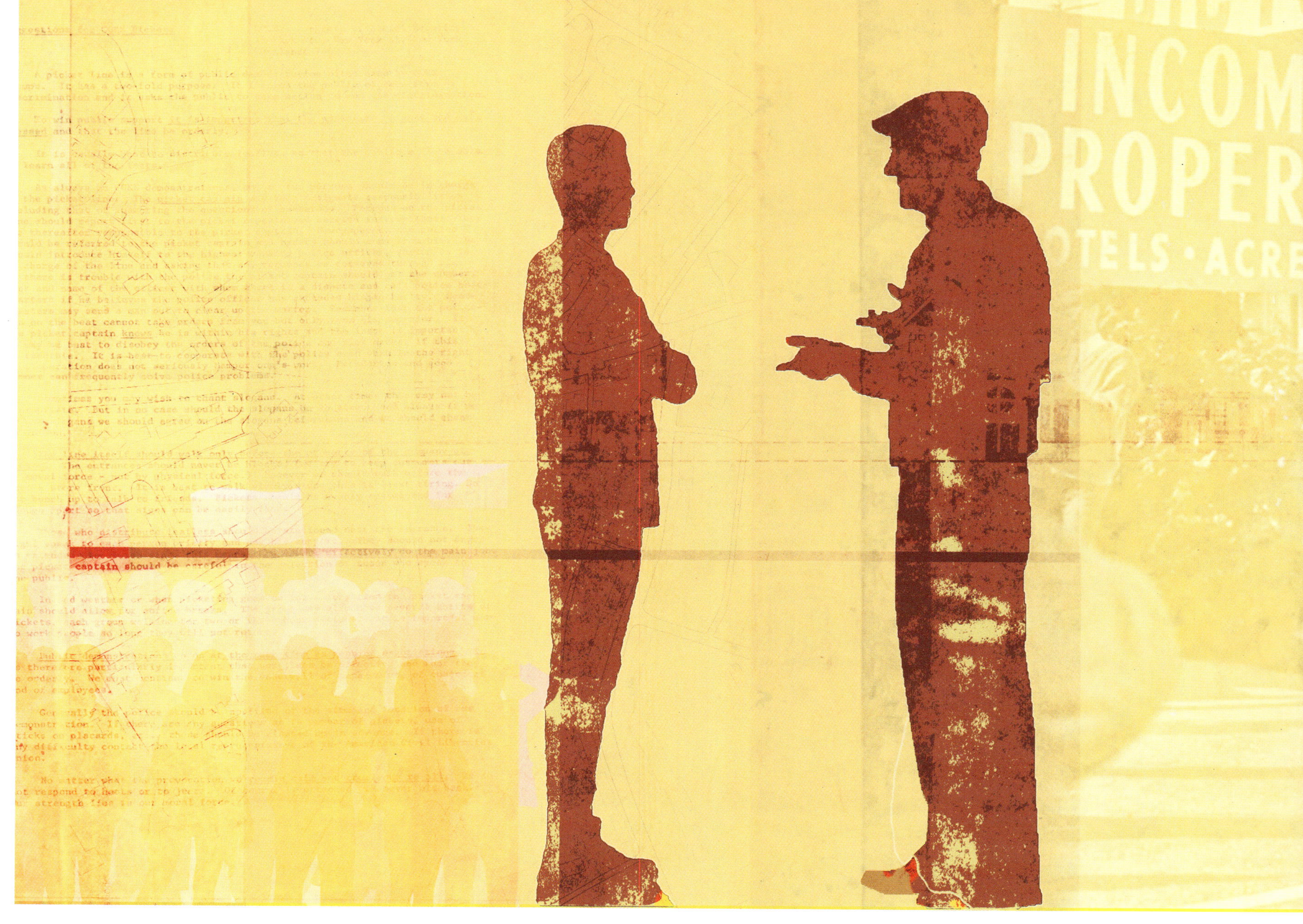

INCOM
PROPER
OTELS · ACRE

WE WERE PART OF CORE

JITE AGBRO
Ed and Joan Singler 2

(Congress of Racial Equality). They were doing a thing called Operation Window Shop.

We went to Ballard because a real estate agency there had ads in the paper for houses.

So my husband and I were the first couple to go in. The real estate gentleman was polite. We had the newspaper and we said, "We'd like to see this particular house." He said, "I'm sorry but that house isn't available."

I said, "Well, can I have your card? He was so glad we were leaving.

Well, there was another couple waiting outside. A white couple.

So we gave them his card and told them to ask for the red–head.

When they asked to see the same house, he took them right to it.

Off they went.

That was kind of sad.

Alice Thomas

I WAS PRETTY SHELTERED

when I was in elementary school. I had a
fantastic fifth grade teacher named Miss
Haugen. She had two dresses, a brown
one and a gray one, and she always
carried a hanky stuffed in the sleeve.
She was a really tough teacher, but she
helped to mold me in a way. She encouraged me to be a great student.

When I got to Sharples Junior High,
which is Aki Kurose now, when I was
about to turn thirteen, I started finally
tuning into what was going on in the
world. This was 1962–63, so by then we
had a color television, and I became more
worldly, paying attention to what was
happening beyond Seattle.

Cleveland High School was a really interesting place for me, because I was want-
ing to push against some authority, by
that point, and ask a lot of questions. We
didn't have a Black Student Union. My
sister was even more of a rabble-rouser

ROMSON BUSTILLO
Stephanie

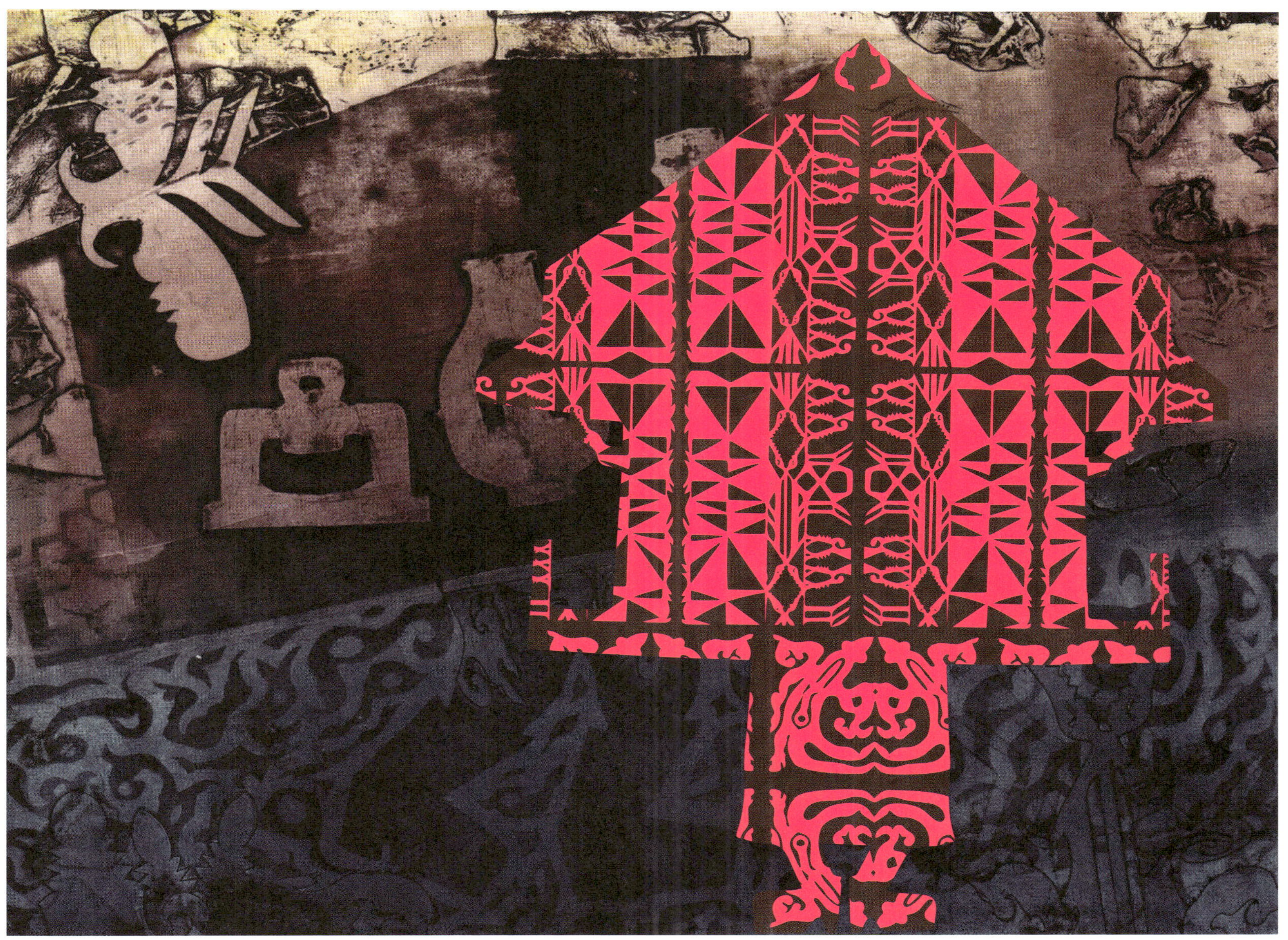

than I was. So she, with three other students, started the Black Student Union at Cleveland High School. We sat in at Cleveland, because they said we could not use a room at the school for our Black Student Union meetings. We had to meet somewhere else and it had to be a certain distance from the school. So we all sat on the floor, and our parents were called, and we were suspended and sent home. That was the first time I saw my mother get so angry. She was using words I hadn't heard before! She went up to the school with the dad of a best friend. Her dad was very active in the NAACP. So he comes up to the school with my mom and just reads the school the riot act, and we did end up getting to use the cafeteria for our meetings after that encounter. From then on, everybody was like, "Your mom is COOL! We love your mom!"

By '69 I was getting ready to head off to college. I wanted to go to The UW, but I got this opportunity to go to Whitman, and oh, boy. It was so conservative, not at all what I had expected. I knew it was a liberal arts school, and I was really encouraged by my mother to accept the scholarships, so I went and I tolerated it for the first year. But, I wanted to be Angela Davis at that time. I wanted to raise my fist and rally. Being one of four Black women on the entire campus, and not even ten Black men, at that time, I didn't have anybody to raise a fist to! I did create a little bit of a ruckus there, and became president of the Independent Women for the first year, but then found my way back to Seattle and to the University of Washington, to the Office of Minority Affairs, where I went to school and worked with Larry Gossett, in the University heydays, when Roberto Maestas was there, and Sam Kelly. We were all aligned and felt like we were doing really good things at The U.

I first met Aaron Dixon during the whole Black Student Union thing at University of Washington with Larry Gossett. I had a friend who lived next door to the Dixons on 34th, up in Madrona. I would go over to her house and both of us, it wasn't just me, we'd sit on the porch and wait for the Dixons to come out. They were rock stars. They'd be wearing the black berets, the black leather jackets, and they would be heading across the street to the park, where they used to march with all of the comrades. And we'd give them the Black power sign, like "Hey, Elmer, Aaron - woo!" That's so embarrassing, when I think back on it now. I think they knew I had a crush on them.

Stephanie Johnson-Toliver

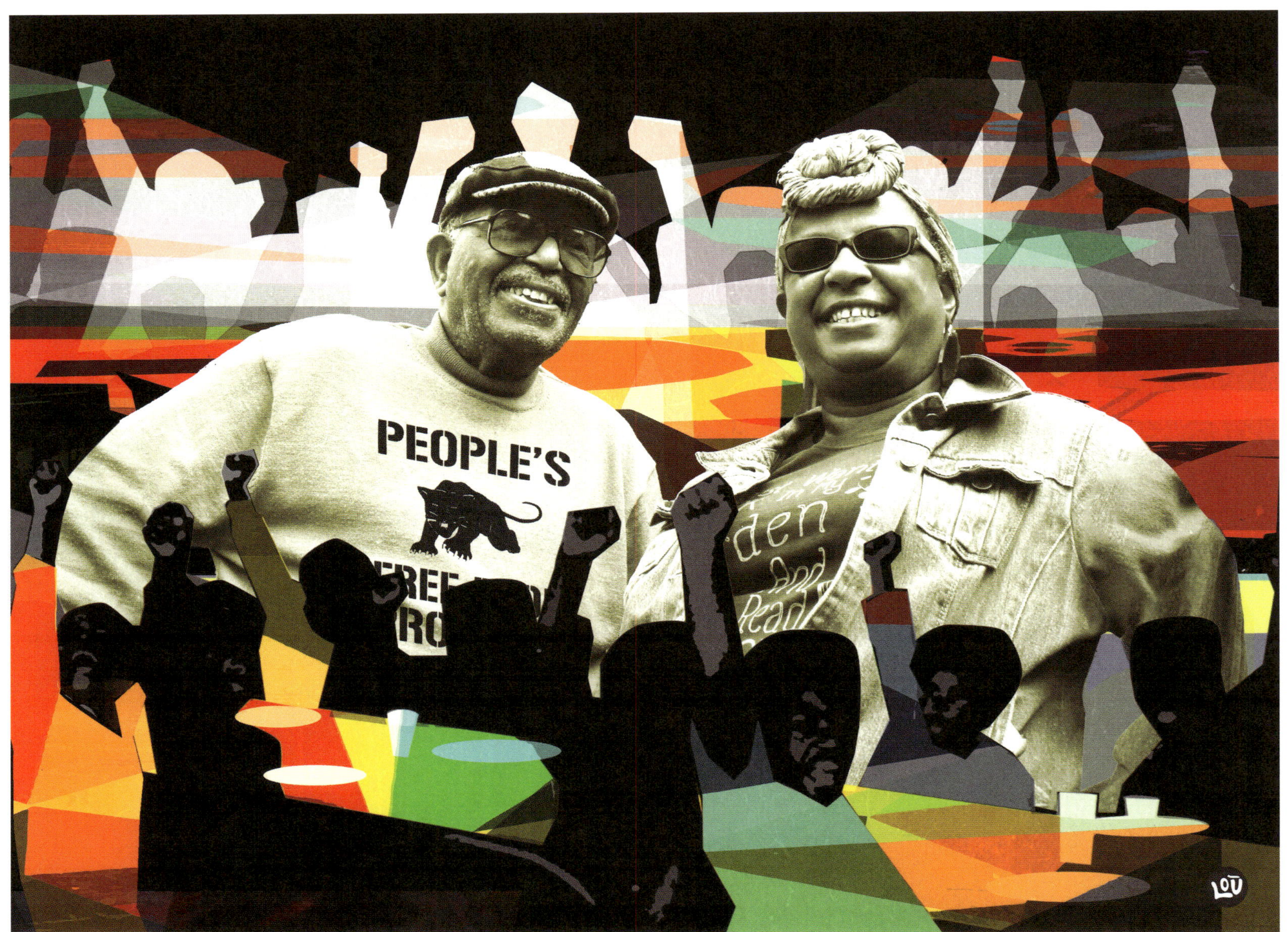

PEOPLE'S
FREE
RO
LOU

CECIL:

What the Panthers actually did was they fed a lot of kids in the mornings, breakfast. I mean they fed tons of breakfast food to kids.

Phyllis Beatty Yasutake: They shamed the country into starting that breakfast program.

And they started Carolyn Downs clinic, a free clinic. Doctors from the University of Washington volunteered to come work there and give people free physicals, check babies, do all that. Then they started the sickle cell testing. My son, Cecil, was like two years old, and it was hard getting information on sickle cell. My son had been diagnosed with it, but nobody was talking about it. People didn't know about it in our community, and the Panthers and the University of Washington doctors trained hundreds of people, gave them kits, and had them go door to door and poke fingers and take blood samples to test them for sickle cell anemia, the trait and the disease. It really educated the community, because people didn't know about it.

Cecil: And they would go to lumber yards and get lumber to fix up people's houses. They'd go to Dunn Lumber, and the owner wouldn't take their money. He was scared. "Just get what you need. You need some more 2 x 4s?" He'd give them all the lumber they'd need and they'd come out and build up people's homes, old folks homes.

Phyllis: They did a lot of community stuff. But they would also carry their rifles and march down 34th. They looked sharp too, in those berets!

DAMON BROWN
Cecil and Phyllis

WE STARTED CLEAN GREENS

because Reverend Jeffrey got sick, and the doctor said
he wasn't eating healthy. So he said, "Well, let's get
some organic food in here."

We do the farm, we bring the produce into the city,
and we sell at reasonable prices so that people can eat
healthy. My daughter said, "Mom, you came from a
farm, why would you want to go out there farming?"
She doesn't understand the fact that I love, I love, I
love farming. I love the dirt, I love to see stuff grow,
and I love how the people enjoy the fresh veggies. A
lot of the people can't wait till we open the market.
And then we do Fresh Bucks. That's where, if you have
an EBT card, you pay for two dollars worth of greens,
and we give you four dollars worth of greens. So it's
double your bucks.

We've been around for ten years with Clean Greens,
and everybody loves it, everybody knows about it,
but we're "not sustainable." That's what the City
of Seattle tells us. We're not sustainable. They say
we're not making any money. We're not in here for
the money. It's needed. Food is needed, good food
is needed.

Lottie Cross

JITE AGBRO
Lottie

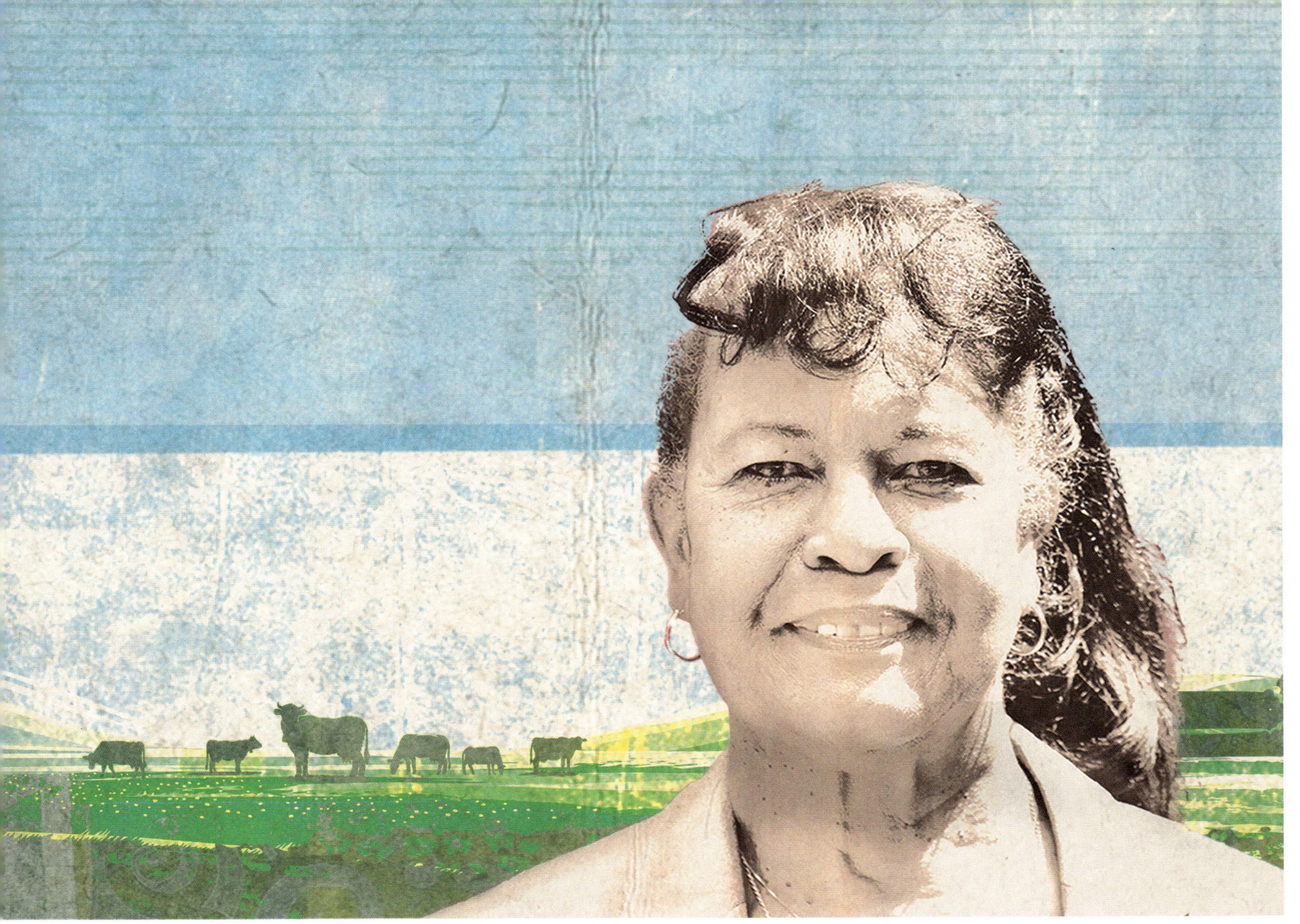

MY NAME IS

Mark Edwin Cook. I was born here, in King County Hospital, about 1936, to a family of eight children. My father died really early, when I was about four years old, so my mother raised us all the way through high school, and she was a domestic worker, over in Bellevue area. My father, when he was alive, was a red cap down at King Street Station. He settled here after he got out of the army.

I remember the 23rd and Yesler library. Every Saturday, all the kids in the neighborhood would go there, and this woman would read stories to us. We'd sit in the children's corner. One of them that they read to me, The Little Red Hen, I carried over to my Black Panther days when I was in prison, in Walla Walla.

Later we moved to Queen Anne. Queen Anne was white. We had three Black families in Queen Anne. I was going to Queen Anne High School.
One day, I had a lot of change in my piggy bank, heavy stuff, so I was going to the school cashier in the cafeteria. I asked, "Could you change this to cash for me?" And she said,

"Sure." One of the adult supervisors came along and said, "No. You don't do nothing for those kind of people."

I just blew up. We had milk bottles made of glass in those days, and I just took it and threw it. It happened to go through a window. This is on the third floor. And so, they kicked me out of school.

When I went home, I told my mother. I was about seventeen years old. I said, "Mom, I want to go in the Air Force, and I need your permission, and I'll pay for everything, believe me." But the next morning, two Seattle police officers were there. They arrested me for third-degree assault.

The judge sent me to Western State Hospital. They said nothing was wrong with me. One doctor told me, "You're not insane. You never have been insane, and you probably never will be insane," but the judge sent me for indefinite commitment. That was a scary place. The experiences there were worse than anything I experienced in adult prisons. They had me chained in bed. That is where I became more anti-authoritarian.

After I got out of the mental hospital, I was looking for work but no one wanted to give me a job, because I'd been in a mental hospital. I tried to enlist, but they said, "He can't go in because he's been in a mental hospital."

So that was the transition, you might call it, from trying to make a living to being a thief.

In prison, five guys came up to me while I was on the prison yard and asked me if I wanted to join them in doing a little journalism. They said, "Now, you can't tell anybody about this. It's going to be a secret paper we're going to write." So we put together an underground newspaper called "The Bomb." And the way we did it, we used stuff we got out of the kitchen. We stole gelatin out of the kitchen, and we got a steel pitcher and two razor blades and some matches, and we made a steamer to boil water in this thing and poured the gelatin in there, and then after it boiled, we poured it on this frame, on a mirror. And when it cooled, we typed on the back of what we called ditto paper

and laid it on that gelatin and smoothed it out, peeled it off, and then took regular paper and put it on and peeled it off, and we had a newspaper going. And it became really popular, trying to get everybody in the prison on the same page, trying to break down racism and everything, and they could never know who was writing it.

And that's the way I sort of made it through prison. That's when I became a Panther and started a Panther chapter inside. I'm a Panther to this day.

I think the most important organizing tool I learned in prison is how important journalism is. When I was working with Panthers at Walla Walla, the Panther Paper allowed organizing between prisoners and other organizations. When I worked with prisoners in California, we printed a newsletter for them. No matter how much antagonism there was between the prisoners, if you could do a newsletter, you could get everyone on the same page. We were able to get 30,000 prisoners together. Journalism is important to making a movement work.

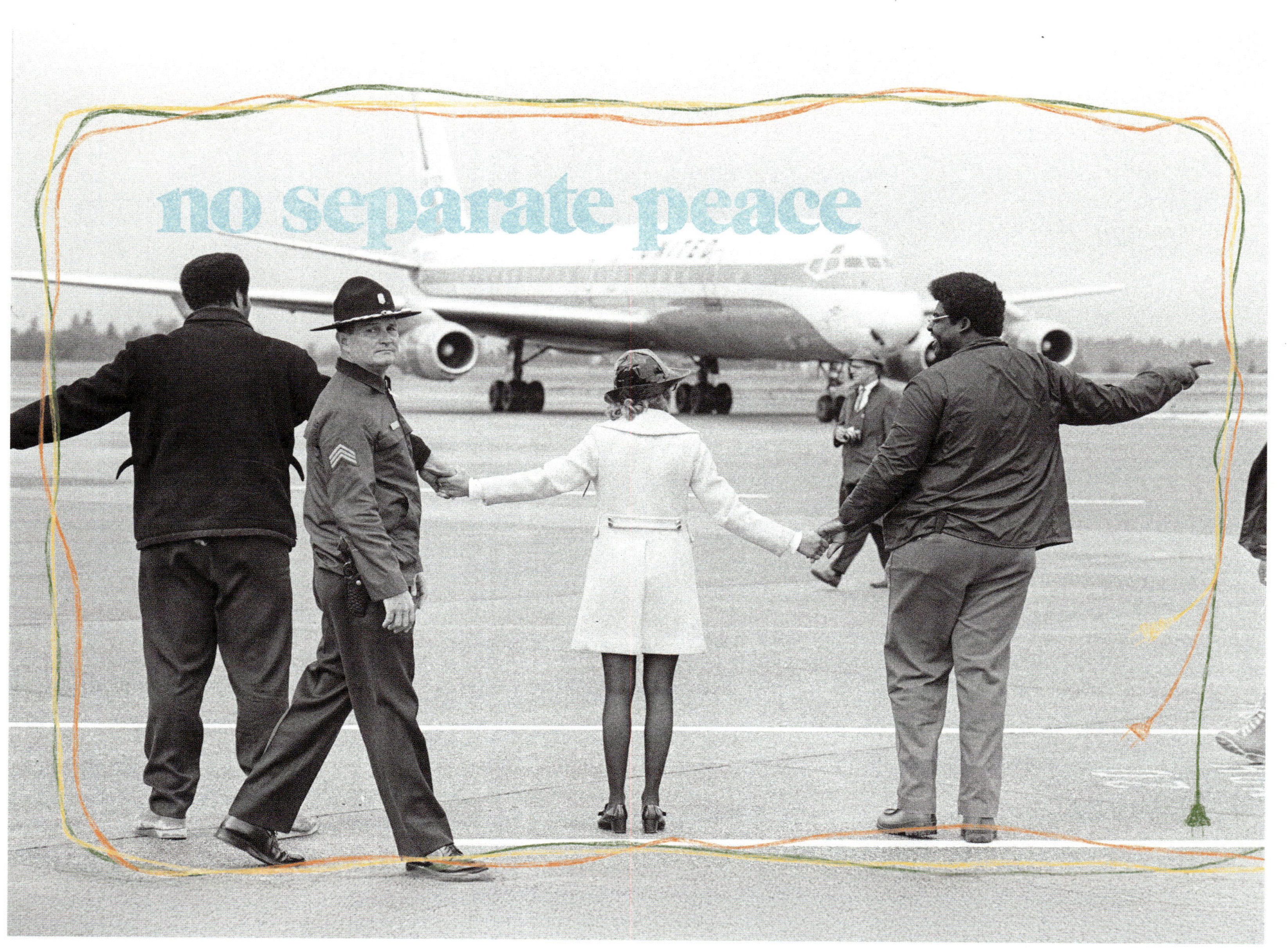

no separate peace

MY NAME IS

ERIN SHIGAKI
Michael Fox

Michael Fox, and I was born in New London, Connecticut, in 1944.

I arrived in Seattle in September of 1969, and I went to work with what was then known as Seattle Legal Services, a civil legal aid organization. It had an office at 24th & Jackson.

Supporting the United Construction Workers was the main thing that I did in the Central Area, and it was an all-consuming task, because this was a major movement in the Central Area, from 1968 really up into the 1980s.

Seth Scott, who maintained an electrical company named Scott Electric, tried to get some public jobs but was told he would have to get his workers from the union, which meant they would be white workers. That started people talking, and the contractors themselves formed an organization called the Central Contractors Association - CCA. The CCA eventually changed into the UCWA, the United Construction Workers Association, when more and more African American workers got involved in this movement.

Tyree Scott, who was Seth Scott's son, had returned to Seattle after being an electrician in the Marines, and it immediately became apparent to him that the skilled trades were almost all white. By skilled trades I mean the electricians, Local 46, the operating engineers, Local 302, the sheet metal workers, Local 99, the iron workers, Local 86, and the plumbers and pipefitters, Local 32. Those unions had a workforce of, probably, a thousand each, and there were fewer than ten African Americans in each of those trades.

So, the tactic they developed was job shutdowns. And these were right out of the Civil Rights Movement playbook. One of their most memorable actions took place at the Medgar Evers pool, which is the public swimming pool adjacent to Garfield High School. That project was being built in 1968, and of course it was named after Medgar Evers, the civil rights hero who was murdered in Jackson, Mississippi. It was, ironically, being built by an all-white workforce, in the heart of the Central Area. More than one hundred African American workers, with hard hats, surrounded that job project and demanded that the job be shut down until they had African Americans employed there.

Another action was the "Shit In At Sea Tac." There was a huge remodeling of the airport underway, and they weren't hiring Black workers. There were more than one hundred people arrested at this action. Somehow more than fifty workers got out on the tarmac, linked arms together, and ran up and down the runway. Planes had to be diverted to Portland. Meanwhile, other actions were taking place inside the airport. Construction workers went into the men's room and all sat down in the stalls. And just stayed there. Nobody could use any of the stalls. So there were people, you know, kind of frantic, about to get on a flight, needing to go to the john, and all the bathrooms were incapacitated.

Several other workers got in the ticket lines and then said, "I'd like to buy a ticket to Dallas, and then from Dallas to Mexico City, and then from Mexico City to Rio de Janeiro, and from Rio de Janeiro to Cape Town, South Africa," and this was before computers, so the ticket agent is writing this all down, and then they get to the end of this request and say, "By the way, how many Blacks do you have working on this construction project here?"

"I don't know."

"Well then forget the whole thing! I don't wanna fly out of here."

In the meantime, the lines for tickets are getting longer and longer.

These were the kind of actions that were taking place all over town. Out of the White House came this direction to the Justice Department, "Do something about this."

So, a task force of FBI agents and civil rights lawyers from the Justice Department arrived in Seattle and started this very aggressive investigation of the building trades. They showed up at the union halls with subpoenas to get hiring records. Then the Civil Rights Division of the Department of Justice filed this case called "United States versus Local 86 et al." It included the five unions that I mentioned plus the joint apprenticeship and training committees that each of the unions had, which were, of course, the avenue for people to get into the unions. This lawsuit was put on a fast track and tried in May 1970. Judge William Lindberg issued a comprehensive injunction requiring the unions to admit Black workers into the apprenticeship programs and to graduate them within a certain period of time. After that, for the next ten years, the major work that UCWA was doing was enforcing the injunction.

In September 1970, there was a series of farmworker wildcat strikes in the Yakima Valley. At the same time, UCWA was doing its work in Seattle, and getting a very solid base in the African American community. There were picket lines, in the Seattle area, to boycott grapes at various grocery stores, and the farmworkers would come over from Yakima to join these picket lines. I can remember very vividly, at the grocery store on MLK, what was then Empire Way, and Union Street, there were probably fifteen farmworkers and, at least, fifteen African American construction workers, with their hard hats on, picketing that grocery store, and nobody went into that store. I mean it was just completely shut down.

A lot of these farm workers were from Mexico and had hardly had any contact with African Americans before. This was a tremendous surprise to them, that there would be this kind of support. It was a liberating experience for them. At the same time, a lot of the African Americans had had no contact at all with Mexicans, certainly not monolingual Mexicans who wore cowboy hats. This repeated itself over the winter. There were more pickets where farm workers came over and African Americans went there, and there was an increasing politicization of the construction workers about this being part of a larger struggle.

Seattle was a pretty conservative place in the '60s and before. The political dynamic of the city has changed since then, and I think a contributing factor was the political organizing of the late '60s and '70s. It had an effect far beyond just getting people construction jobs. And Tyree Scott, a real leader in all of this organizing, was one of the most influential people in my life. He was a genius in terms of organizational tactics. He was also an extraordinarily funny man, probably the best storyteller I ever heard. He knew how to relate to everybody. He was a great negotiator.

AW MAN, TYREE SCOTT

I was an up-and-coming organizer, and I was doing an internship at American Friends Service Committee, in Philadelphia, and there was an organizer there by the name of Micheal Simmons who said, "If you're an up-and-coming organizer, you need to know Tyree Scott."

He was just an amazing human being. I mean, I learned so much from him. He always talked about the importance of struggle. He says, "You can't throw people away. We don't like to struggle with each other, and it's important that we do, because struggling helps you get better."

Tyree was a health nut, and I wasn't. I like fries, hamburgers. Whenever I would get in trouble, Tyree would take me out to the healthiest place, and he wasn't the type to chastise you. He would tell you, in a story, why what you did was wrong. He'd be telling me a story. He had such a big heart, and he loved people so much. Tyree was always about struggle. He wasn't about force; he was about persuasion. Sometimes now when things are difficult and hard, I think, "What would Tyree do? What would Tyree say?"

KL Shannon

MAMA KRAMER

She started out being really active in CORE, but she left CORE because she didn't think they were radical enough. She really got into Pan Africanism and Black Nationalism and became a book vendor. She was Seattle's main source for Black intellectual material. She was responsible for connecting Seattle's Black consciousness community with the larger national and international community. She would bring Black intellectuals and authors and academics to Seattle. People talk about the Dixon brothers, and we know about the Gang of Four, but what about all the people that created the intellectual and ideological environment in which those people could coalesce their actions; the people who created a community base that allowed those people to be the vanguard? Mama Kramer just really jumps out at me as one of those people.

Inye Wokoma

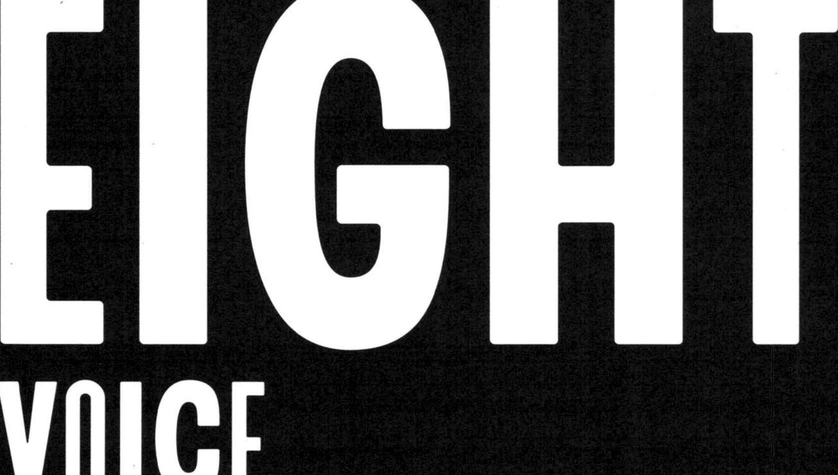
EIGHT
VOICE

Antwone Fisher stands alone in a field, looking across at a barn. Magically he is transported to its opening doors where he is greeted by a towering man who, with a warm smile and safe hands, leads him inside to a towering woman who takes him even deeper into the barn. The barn is a sanctum and running its length is a table laden with every delicacy a child could imagine. Surrounding the table are countless people, Antwone's family extending back generations. They are silent and smiling, a host of guardian angels. At the head of the table Antwone is seated before a stack of impossibly sumptuous buttered pancakes. The moment ends abruptly with an adult Antwone waking from his dream.

When I reminisce about my childhood in the Central District. I often think about our Black radio station, KYAC. My memories of the community and the radio station are like Antwone's dream, a safe place with a large table, surrounded by every person imaginable, and laden with the most impossibly sumptuous meal. I grew up listening to KYAC, soul music, church sermons and gospel music, talk shows, commercials for Black businesses, deejays, call in contests, request lines, and again the music, always the magical, never-ending stream of

Black music. The voices coming across those airwaves were my neighbors, shopkeeps, teachers. They were the people sitting next to me on the bus and the people driving past me as I gazed out my living room window. KYAC unlocked the doorways of my own imagination and allowed me to step into the lands and lives of Black people in far away places. Places I had never been, but heard about daily in the conversations of the adults around me. When I looked to the east, and the Cascade Mountains felt like a barrier separating Seattle from the rest of Black America, KYAC dissolved those walls and made Seattle feel like everywhere. For a daydreamy, introverted little boy that radio station was a portal to the multiverse.

I was born in 1969. I was a little boy emerging into self-awareness when KYAC was at its height. KYAC went off the air abruptly in 1981. There was a wholeness that I felt listening to KYAC, a sense of belonging and expansiveness that was suddenly lost. It was a shock, like waking from Antwone's dream. KYAC made being Black in Seattle feel universal. I would love to go to sleep and wake up to that feeling again, if only for one day.

Inye Wokoma

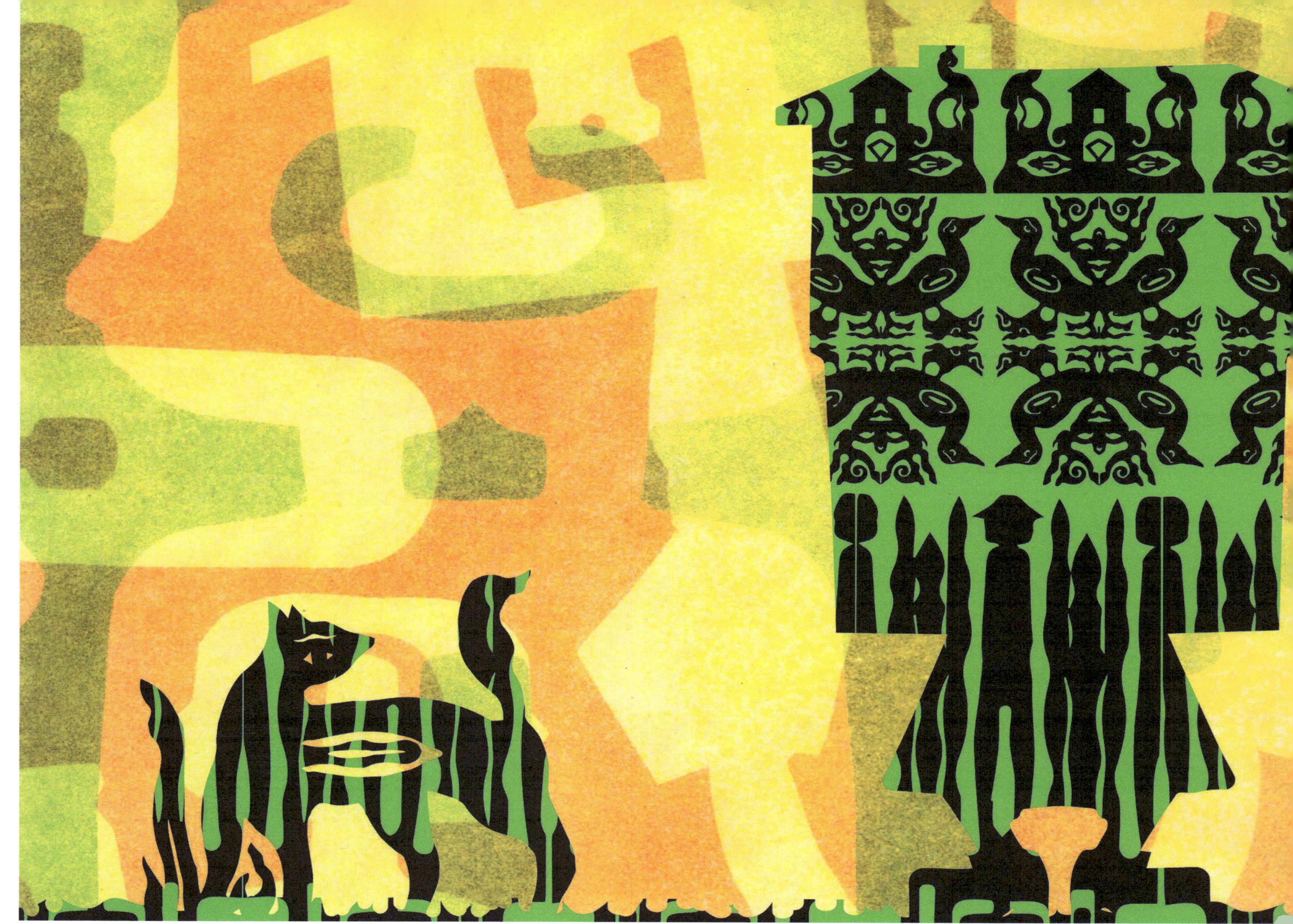

EVERYONE IN MY FAMILY

is originally from Arkansas. My father moved the family to Seattle, in 1952. He arrived in Seattle as a Pullman porter on a train that went from Minneapolis to Vancouver, BC. And then he had three sisters that moved to Seattle, one at a time, after he came.

Eventually my father moved from being a Pullman porter to becoming a merchant seamen. He had a third grade education and saw the world and was one of the smartest men I ever knew. My mother was a seamstress and a tailor. She worked in a really small little shop in Pioneer Square where they made leather jackets for motorcycle policemen. Because I didn't have any sisters, and

my youngest brother was a lot older than me, radio was my companion all the time. The Black station, KZAM, became KYAC, and it was located on 14th and Madison. I would go over whenever I had a chance and just hang out. At nineteen, I got a radio operator's license. I was an engineer, and broadcast communication became my thing.

When I worked there, KYAC had two frequencies, 96.5 FM and 1460 AM, and that's when we were the most powerful. The radio station really saw itself as an extension of the community, truly, which means that we came out into the community. I did my show from Safeway on a number of occasions, and it was cool because I'd be in the window on 23rd. People could see you. They would come into the store. It was good for the store. It was good for the radio station. We would do our radio show in the record store right off of 23rd on Jackson, and when the Whispers came to Seattle, they would come and we would be on the air together. All the people in the community could come on the air and talk about whatever was pressing in the community.

When we lost our Black radio station that's when our community really started to dissipate in my view. We didn't have a compass. There was no way of communicating easily what was happening, not just in Seattle, but in Black communities across the country. I think it was a time where we were really lost. We were out here disconnected. It changed everything.

We also had a Saturday morning television program on KOMO. It must have been late '60s, early '70s. Eddie Rye, Veltry Johnson, Joan Houston, and Lee Carter all anchored this noon television program, and I was a production assistant. They all had these big Afros. And I'm going to tell you, the name of the program was Aggin News. What does Aggin spell backwards? We were on the ABC affiliate with the Aggin News. Nobody was the wiser. I didn't realize until after the fact, actually, just how groundbreaking that really was. We were killing it.

Vivian Phillips

KYAC WAS A REAL HUB

A real key. The beauty of it was that you got your music, and you got talk shows, information. Everybody knew what was going on. It was such a connective thing there. And then when it left, it all just fell apart. All of sudden the community did not have that voice. It's a shame that happened.

Al Doggett

I REMEMBER THE FIRST TIME

I heard The Sugarhill Gang, I was coming down that hill with my mom, and "the hip the hop, and the hibby to hip hop hop, you don't stop." I went, "Damn!" and that changed my life, you know? KYAC was a focal point. That was a beautiful time in this community. The death of KYAC was a death in the family. Seattle, Washington, with no Black radio station. I remember, they had a funeral for KYAC. They marched a casket down 23rd and Union. It was like a death in the family.

Gregory Scott

MY NAME IS

Frank P. Barrow. I got into radio in the tenth grade, in my hometown of Durham, North Carolina. I was head of the high school broadcasting club, I'd do the school announcements, play the national anthem, all that stuff. *Jet* magazine had a picture of a Black radio DJ named Gordon Dewitty, and he worked at KZAM, which was an African-American station in the Seattle area at that time. I saw that and said, "It's time for you to go out to Seattle and see what's happening out there." I graduated high school in '62. Three or four weeks later, I was sitting in Seattle. I didn't know anyone.

I worked at KYAC radio from '68 to '73. I was a radio announcer. Then along the way, I became program director and music director. The station had white ownership at the start. There was a strike. We said, "We're closing it down until we get what we want." And then Don Dudley came along and he had the money to put behind it, so we took the station over.

Basically we were the only African American owned station, and we were playing Black music that people wanted to hear. Music that Top 40 stations would not touch at the time. We played local Black artists. We had a lot of local acts and they appeared at the festivals. We interviewed them over the air and played their music: Black and White Affair; Cold, Bold and Together; Acapulco Gold; Cooking Bag.

Seattle was a segregated city with segregated media. The other local stations, when they sent someone into the CD, they'd treat it like it was a foreign territory. But on KYAC, Black people communicated with Black folks. People would call us sometimes before they would call the police, okay? They'd let us know, "This thing is happening over here. Could you check into it?" And we'd talk about it on the air, we'd send our news reporters out.

We'd broadcast from grocery stores, maybe from an auto dealership on a Saturday afternoon. We did dances at the high schools and at places like the Russian Center, Yesler Terrace, Rainier Vista, Holly Park.

KYAC went off the air because there wasn't enough advertising money. When the Central District lost KYAC, it lost a voice.

KYAC, YEAH

I mean, it was one station, and you listened to it. I listened to Vivian Phillips on the radio. And then years later I get to meet her. And we worked together for years. I mean, that was the only way you could communicate about what was going on. The radio had the ear of the community. When that left, for us to do things, especially with entertainment, it was really disjointed for a long time. I know when I was trying to do things in the '80s, do shows and plays, I really missed the radio.

Steve Sneed

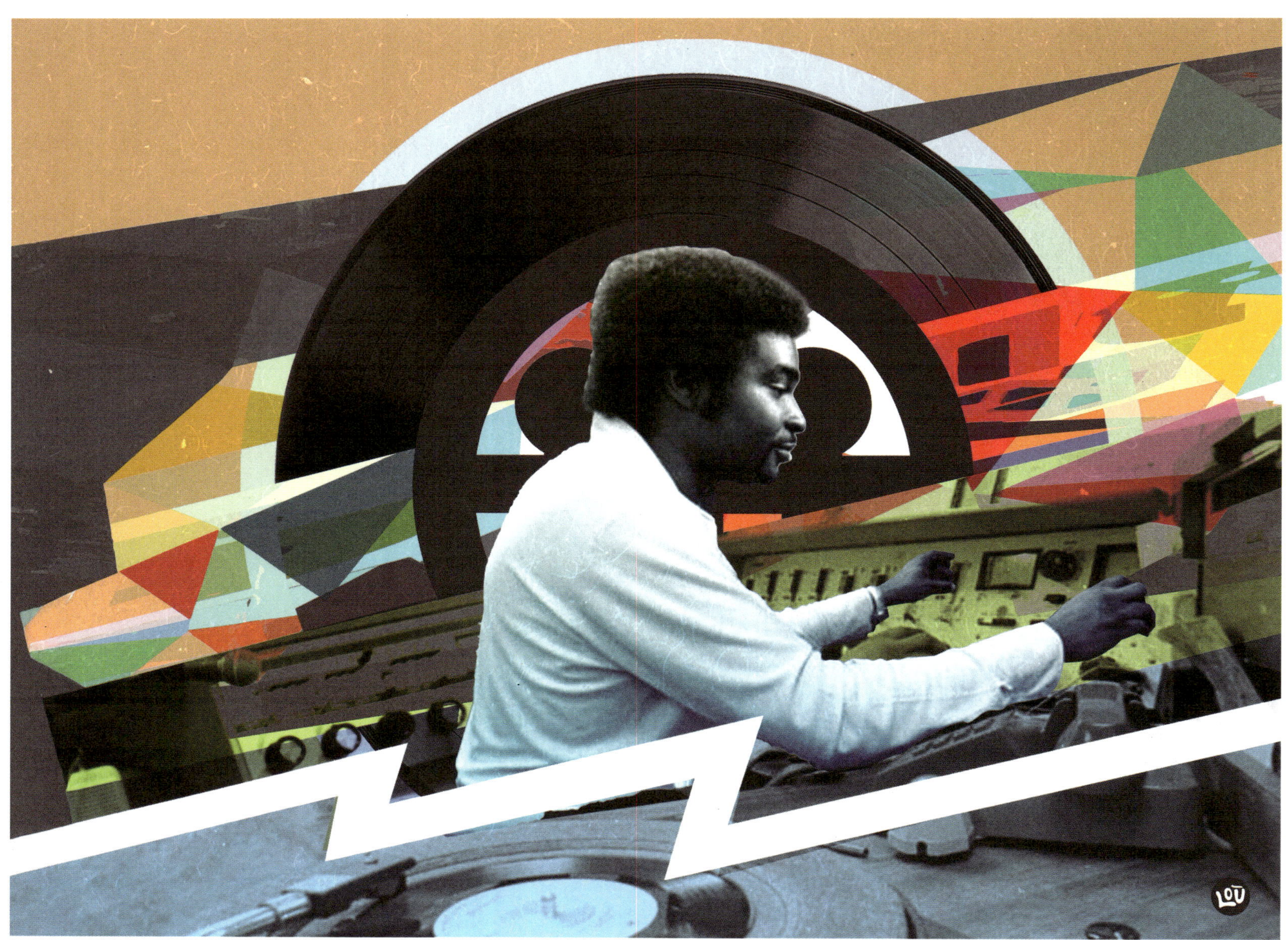

MY NAME IS

DAMON BROWN
KYAC

Leon Carter, and I was born in 1942. I was raised, until I was twelve years old, in Chicago, where I got in trouble and got sent to reform school for doing all those things little boys raised on the street in Chicago do. I finally had to join the army to get off the street. I was stationed with soldiers who were always screaming about how much they loved Fort Lewis and Seattle.

When I was discharged from the army, I got a job with Northwest Airlines, and they offered me a position in Seattle. I came here on June 22, 1968. I never will forget that date. Met my wife one week later. We were married that November.

My aunt was a gospel radio host in Fresno, California. I was impressed, you know? And people had always said that I had a voice for radio. So I started getting interested in broadcasting. I was still working with Northwest Airlines when I ran into the guy who was the news director at KYAC, Veltry Johnson. I loved his voice. He had such a distinct delivery. So I said, "Hey, man, how do I get into this? How do I do this?"

A couple days later he introduced me to the owner, Don Dudley. I told him I could write a news story and I didn't need to get paid, just let me get the experience. He says, "I'll pay you seventy-five dollars a week. But if you apply to the Urban League's on-the-job-training program, they would pay you another seventy-five dollars a week, giving you one-hundred-fifty dollars a week." Well, heck, I'm making five-hundred dollars a week at Northwest Airlines, and I got a baby. Why would I want to do that? Absolutely, yeah, I want to do that. I started there at one-hundred-fifty a week, quit my job at Northwest, and that's how I got into the business.

KYAC was essential. I mean, it was the hub. I interviewed so many celebrities, Stokely Carmichael, Julian Bond, Angela Davis. They all came to Seattle. The arts scene was booming. It was just an extraordinary time. I remember one time Roberto Maestas came running into my house and he grabbed me and hugged me. The occupation of the building that became El Centro de la Raza was going on, and I had done a radio story on it, and he said he never felt so proud. He was in tears.

As a matter of fact, I was hired directly from KYAC to KIRO radio as news director, and I was the first African American news director at KIRO. The thing I liked about radio was its anonymity. Except for Aggin News! We did that on Channel 4 television, with Nate Long. He got grants to train people like me in TV. Aggin News. We had that joke on Seattle for two years. A–G–G–I–N. Spell it backwards. That's what Aggin News was. We had fun with that.

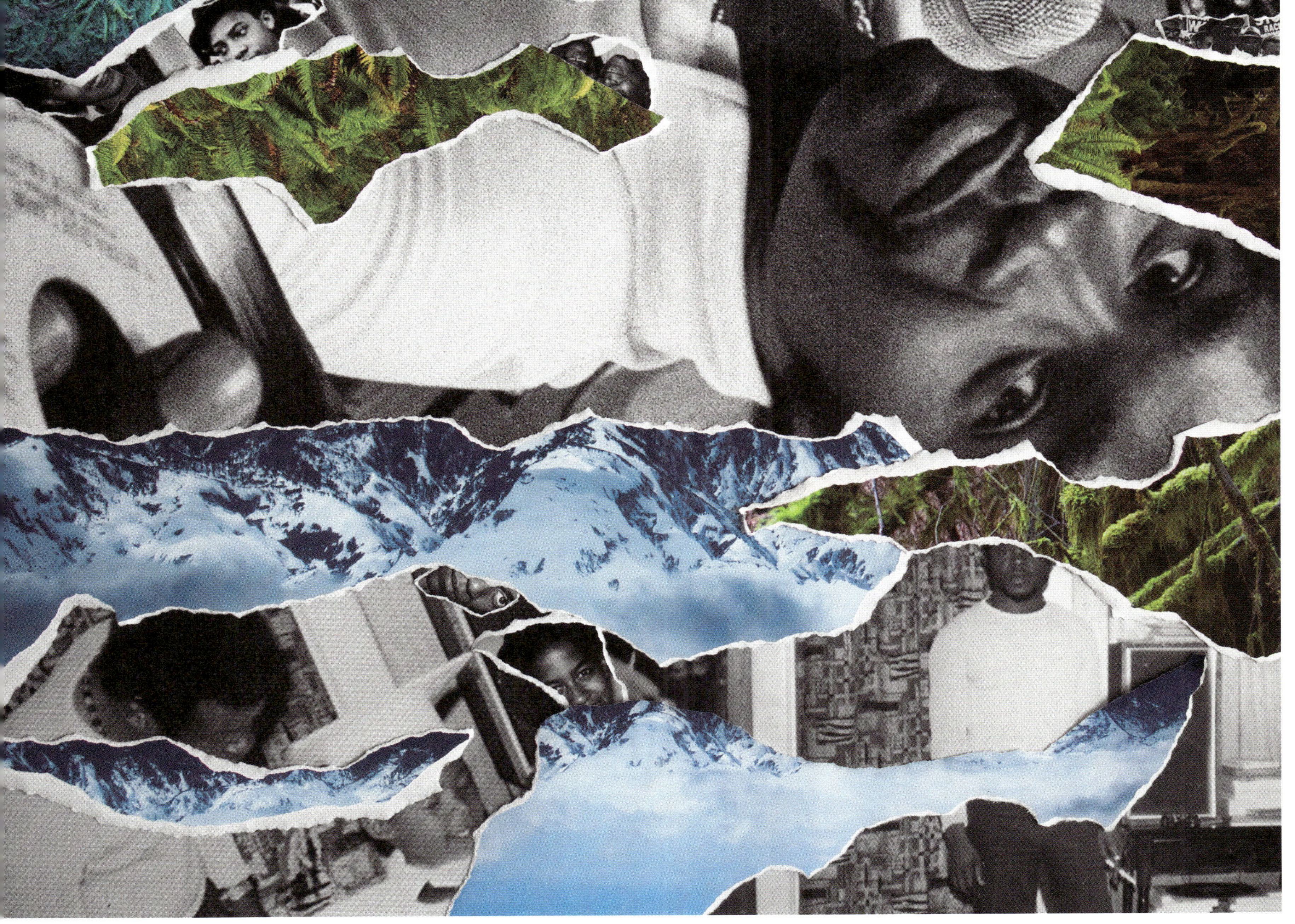

MY NAME IS

Donald Dudley. I was born in Pittsburgh, Pennsylvania, in 1935.

I came here with the army. I landed at Fort Lewis from Fort Chaffee, Arkansas. Troopship. It was March and it was raining. I went to sleep in the barracks when it was dark and wet. But when I got up the next morning, sun was shining, and I opened the door, and there's this big ice cream cone!

Mount Rainier! I was captured!

My aunt was the first woman to have her own radio show, in Pittsburgh. Her program was called Moving Around with Mary D. And she actually bought a record store that she ran in Pittsburgh, in the heart of the Black community. And her brother became the first African American anchor at ABC. I was a frequent visitor and he'd take me around and introduce me to everyone, and it was fascinating.

So I ended up getting into radio because of the strike at KYAC.

At that time, I had been the first Black manager at King broadcasting, and I was the business and advertising manager for Seattle Magazine.

So the white ownership of KYAC came to me to help them get out of this strike. They wanted me to come in and meet with the employees, and I refused.

I said, "I need to understand their issues before I volunteer to come in." But then they sent a message to my secretary that they needed me to come by the studio for an emergency.

When I arrived, all the employees were there, and I was being introduced as somebody who had agreed to help.

They tricked me into coming in.

So I ended up listening to the workers' grievances. The white owners said to me, "We really need you to come be the general manager of the station."

And I said, "What good is that gonna do me?"

They said, "We'll give you an option to buy it."

They never expected me to exercise that option, but I did, right before the end of the first year. I bought the station and took over as general manager. They never expected me to come up with that money.

I was the first African American to control a broadcast license on the West Coast.

At that time, no Black music was played on any white station. And you weren't going to get any information about what was going on with the Black community anywhere in the world. Local Black music made it because of the presence of something like KYAC. That's the only way bands got introduced so they could sell records.

But, we paid the bills with local advertising. We never got the national dollars. We couldn't afford to stay on the air. One of the things my dad always said to me was, "A good run is better than a bad stand." You do the best you can, but if you're getting your butt beat, you better get outta there!

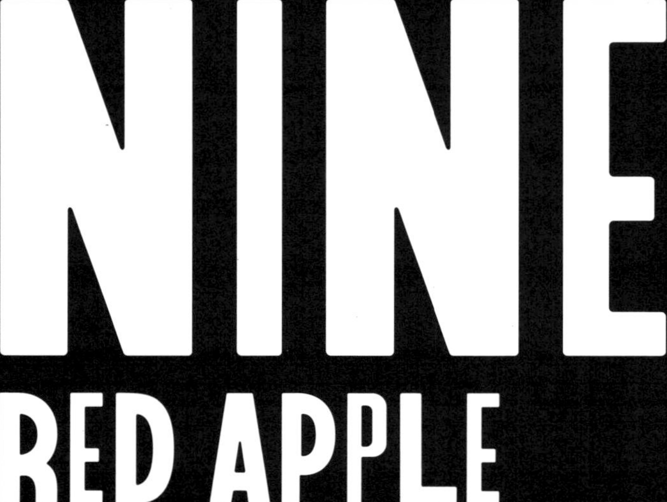

NINE
RED APPLE

Whenever I think of home, I think of the
Red Apple. The Red Apple is what it means
to come home for me.

Aretha Basu

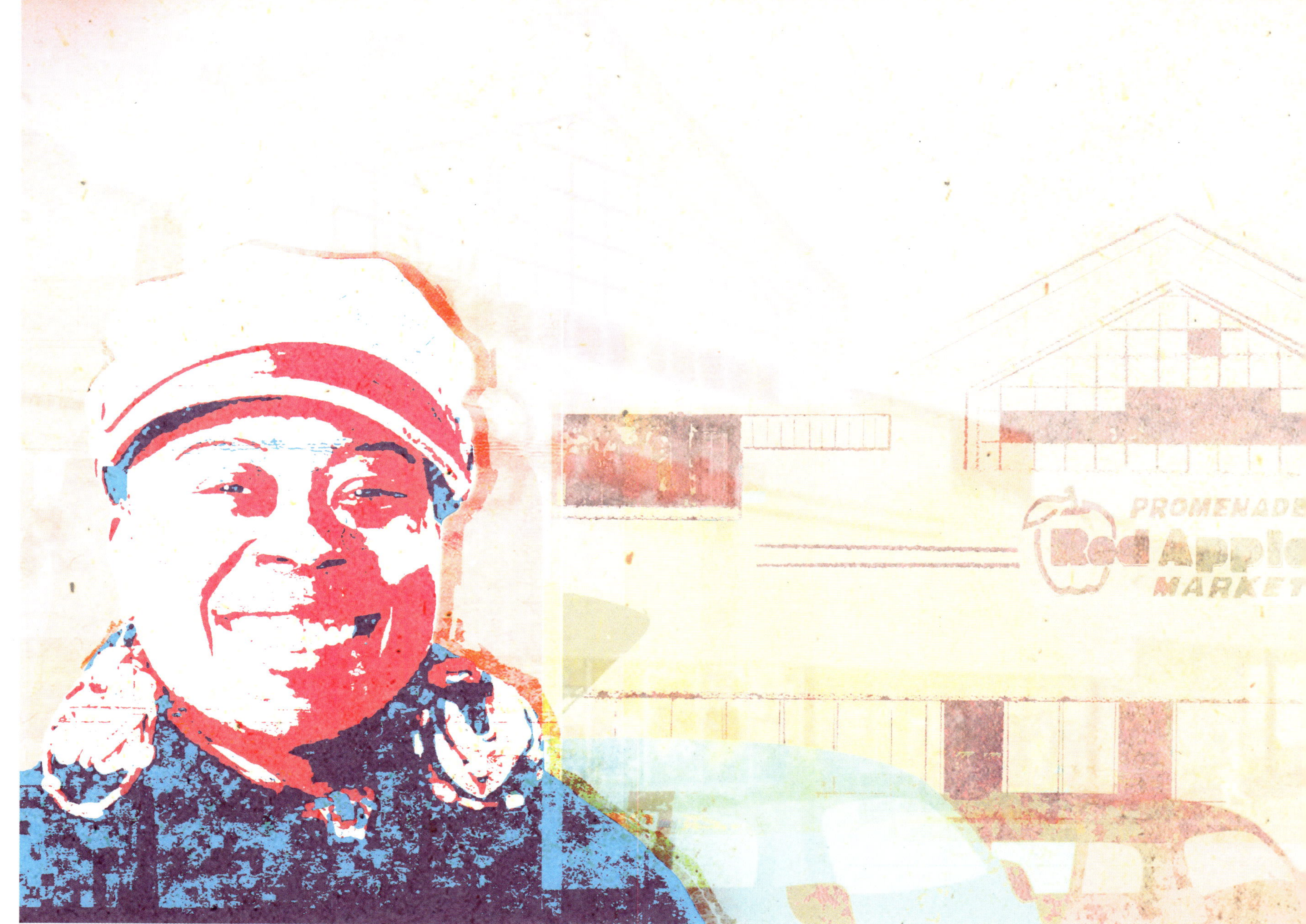
PROMENADE
Red Apple
MARKET

MY NAME IS

Kristi Brown, and I was born in 1970, in Kansas City, Missouri.

My dad was a Pullman porter in college, so he would take the train up here and he loved it. Then my mom came up here to visit and she fell in love with it, so then we were moving. My mom worked for the archdiocese in Kansas City, so she transferred up here, and we moved to Renton.

When we moved here, we didn't know where to shop for our food, and everybody was like, "Oh yeah, you just have to go to the Promenade, the Red Apple." So that's where we came. It was just immediate really. We needed cornbread and we needed ham hocks, so we came to the Red Apple, and we were super, super glad to be here, like super glad. We hadn't seen any Black people. I remember being like, "Hi, how are you, Hi, hi. Hey, Black people. Hi Black people!" And they were looking at us like we were the strangest thing. But we didn't care. We did not care.

Years later, I had a catering business, and then I started making black eyed pea hummus. After thirty people tell you, "You should put that in the grocery store," that is a message. I came into the Red Apple and was like, "I have this product and I want somebody to taste it."

They sent me to the deli and she tasted it. "That stuff is good. We like that."

So, they were my first store that I was in, and that was everything. That was everything.

My mom died in '06. When I tell you that we walked up to Black people, like "Hi, how are you," when we first moved here, that was real. That was me and my mom. So to come back and be able to have my product in that store, it was such a big deal, and they had no idea.

JITE AGBRO
Kristi Brown

THERE'S A LADY

that works over there, June. I been knowing June since I moved to Seattle.

June worked at Red Apple. For. Ever. Love June to death.

Every year I do my teen musical program, and the kids come up to the Red Apple from Langston Hughes, and June will call me.

"We got some kids up here, Isiah, acting real bad, and I know they're part of your program 'cause I just asked them what're they doing and they were like 'We're at Langston this year' and they didn't think I knew you, so I just had to call you."

Those kids were like, *"Isiah won't know that white lady at the Red Apple. Why would he know her?"*

Right? But boom, she'll call, and I'll come up.

Literally if I walk into Red Apple whenever June's working, I don't care who she's taking care of, we stop and give a hug. And I'm gonna tell you now, Red Apple catfish outdoes everybody's catfish. My aunt who cooks for our church, she will only buy her rolls from Red Apple. Whatever celebration we're having, pastor's anniversary or whatever it is, we're gonna have rolls, they're Red Apple rolls, that my aunt bought, of course that she put her pound of butter in.

Isiah Anderson

I GREW UP RIGHT BETWEEN

the Odessa Brown Clinic and SVI, in the apartments between Jackson and Yesler. And growing up, this Red Apple was like the kick-it spot for us. Every Friday, my two best friends Ingrid and Melissa and I had this thing called Hot Cheeto Friday, where we would collect all of our money and come to this Red Apple and buy Hot Cheetos, and then we'd go back to our apartment and climb the side of our building and sit on the roof and just start talking about boys and school and life and family stuff. And we'd eat three bags of Hot Cheetos every Friday. Now my childhood feels like it's closed, really, because there are clerks there who've known me since I was a young kid. They used to tease me about all the candy that I was buying or all the junk food that I was buying. Now I buy vegetables.

Aretha Basu

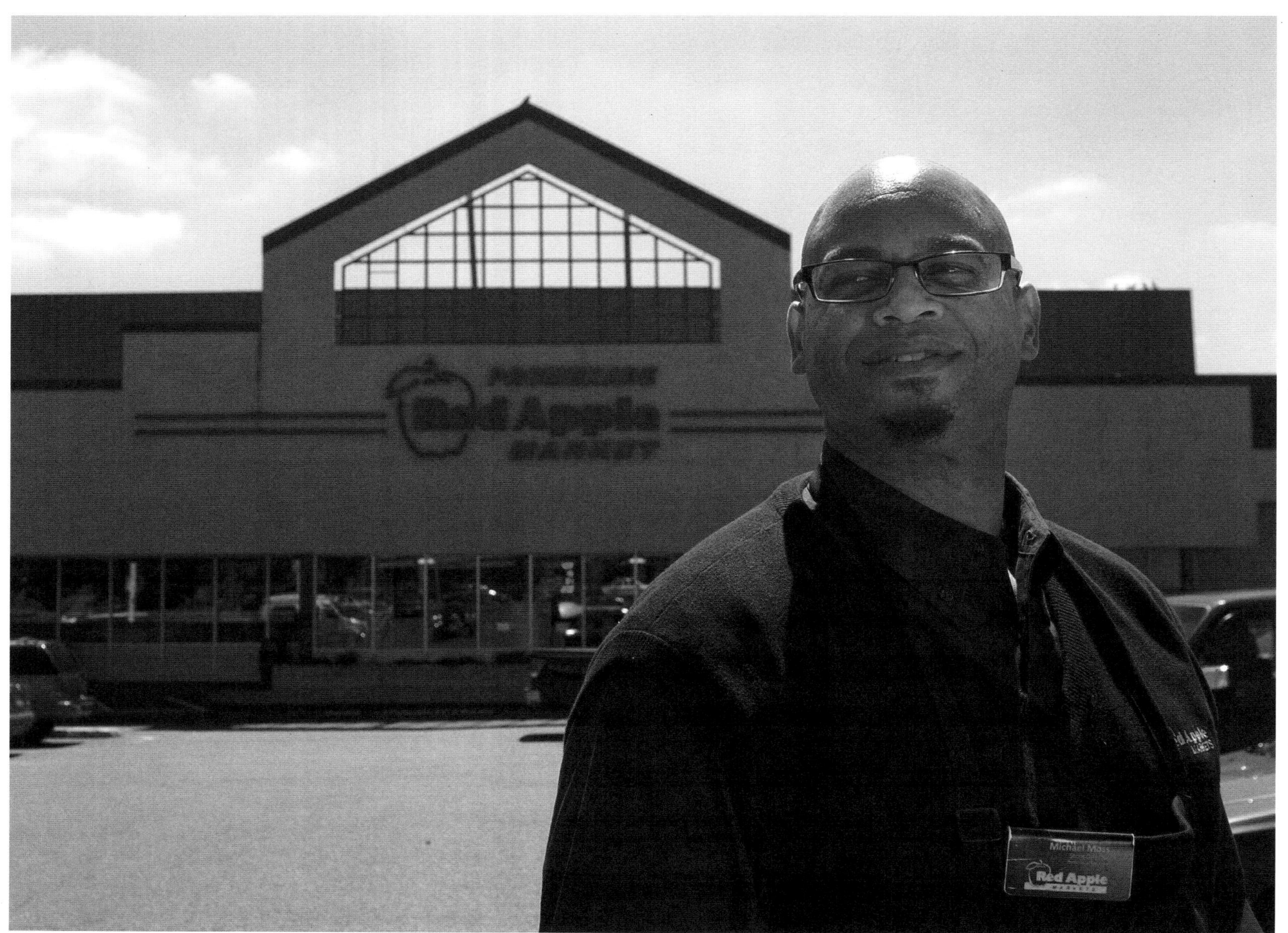

Red Apple
Michael Moss
Red Apple

I LOVE MY JOB.

I worked for another company for a lot of years, and it was all business business business, and then when I came to the Red Apple, the owner, Mr Lenny Rose, he grew up in the neighborhood, he said, "I don't pull any punches, you're a young Black man, this is a Black neighborhood, I want you in this neighborhood, and I want you to connect with this neighborhood. I didn't hire you to just sell groceries, so I'll give you a lot of time to do things for the neighborhood."

I was pretty young. I was thirty-one, I believe. The first day I worked there, I was in the back room, and we had some white managers that were working for me, and they run to the back room and tell me, "We gotta get up front, we gotta get up front!" And I'm like—"What's going on?"

Well the kids were about to get out of school. Now, if you've ever been at the Red Apple when the middle school or the high school gets out, we get flooded with children. Well, the white managers would line up in all the aisles and stare at the kids.

I was like, "Look, all you guys, go to the back," because I know if I was a kid, and I were to witness that, I'm stealing! You know what I mean? If you're gonna accuse me, I might as well steal. So I opened up a bag of candy, and I gave every kid that walked by me a piece of candy, every day, for about two weeks, I would stand up there and I would throw candy at all the kids.

The biggest challenge was retraining the attitudes of the people that were working there, especially attitudes about young Black children. It was tough, but I continued just to push, push, push, and treat people like people and not like criminals.

Mike Moss

PHOTO BY
INYE WOKOMA

MY NAME IS

Roberto Amaral, but everyone calls me Chuy. I was born in Tepic, Nayarit, in 1979. I've been working at the Red Apple for sixteen years.

I was eight years old when we moved here from Mexico. You come here and you're just muted, you know. You don't know anybody, you can't speak to anybody, and at that time there were a lot of other people, like Vietnamese, Pacific Islanders, Filipinos, but there were no Mexicans. So yeah, muted is the word.

My first job at Red Apple was to come in at six in the morning and clean the bathrooms and mop the floors. That was it. I was eighteen. Now I am a night manager, but I've also worked produce, I cashier, I stock, I do ordering, if the plumbing needs something, I do that.

Red Apple is like a community, you know? It's a community store. Sometimes, for the holidays, customers bring us meals from their homes, or we have little kids bringing us drawings that they drew for us. I actually have one in my drawer still, but she drew it maybe eight years ago, and that little girl is all grown up now. We get a lot of Mexicans who used to live in the neighborhood, and now they're living maybe in Burien or Federal Way. They just got priced out. They still come up, because here they can find the menudo meat or the stuff for tacos de lengua. Sundays they come in, with their families, everybody all grown up. And we have a lot of African Americans that come in from far away to go to church. So Sunday is the big day.

There's this woman, and she has a son who is autistic, and they come to Red Apple every day. They buy a pie! Every day. Her son has a hard time with a lot of stuff, but he likes pies. Sometimes she doesn't have enough money and he doesn't understand that; he just wants the pie. So sometimes the cashier will complete the money. Most days he gets his pie. Think about that, think how hard it'll be for that kid you know, to go there and not have that... *(crying)*.

ROMSON BUSTILLO
Chuy

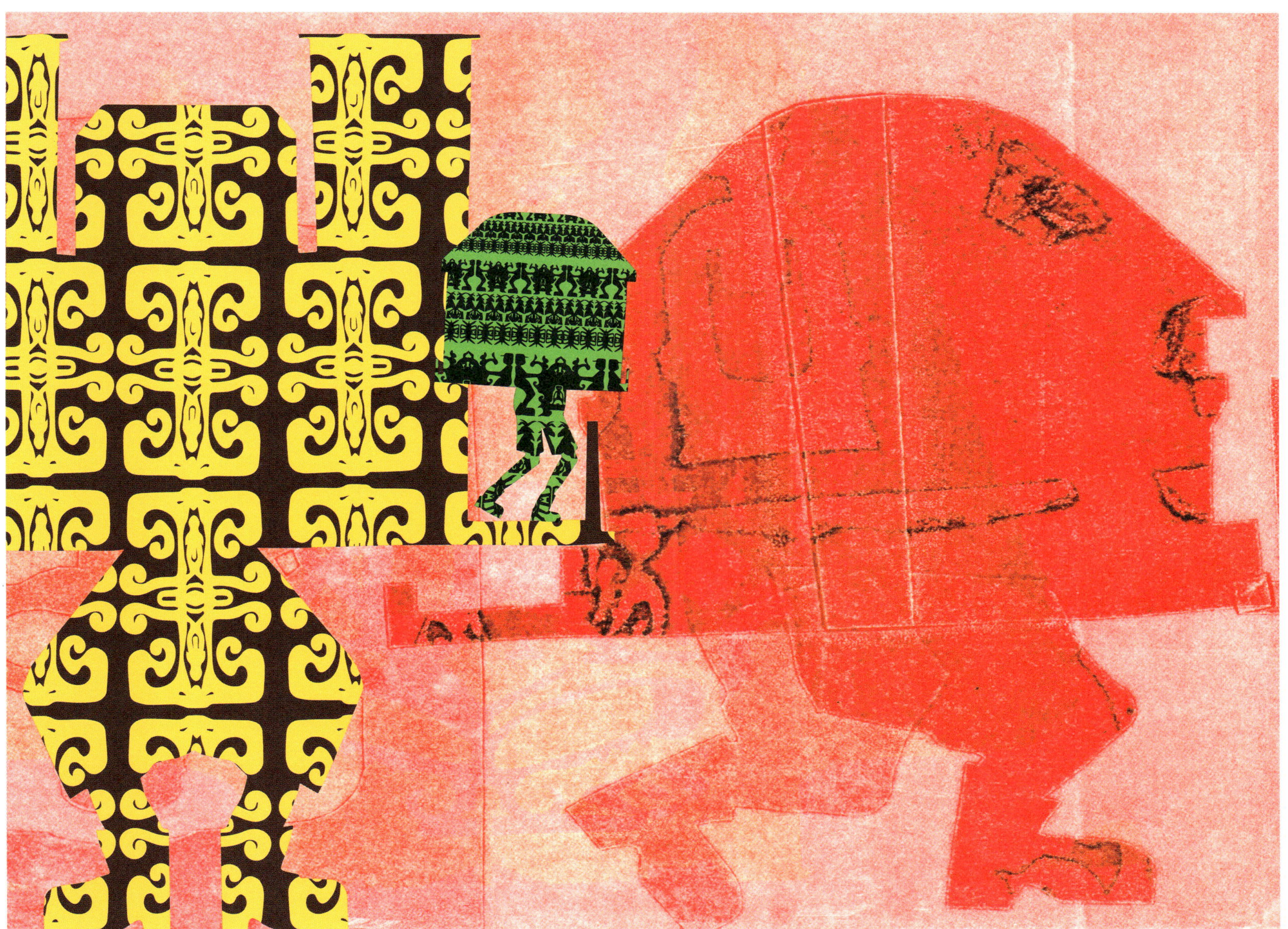

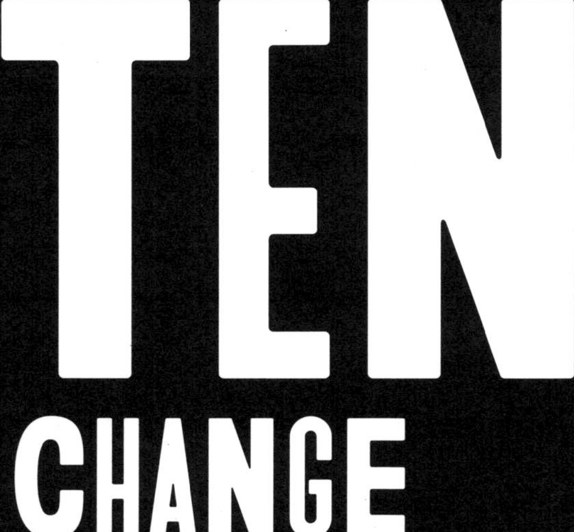

TEN
CHANGE

I struggled with whether or not to
include this chapter because it is mostly
a chapter about loss. What we're doing
with this book is sharing stories about
the creativity, interdependence, resistance, and self-determination that
defined a neighborhood, not engaging in
"gentrification porn." Shelf Life never
set out to portray generations of Central
District residents as victims.

But the reflections in this chapter do
speak to what is lost when communities
are forced to the outskirts. These reflections speak to those of us who might
pass a neighbor without greeting them or
might call the police on someone's child.
These reflections ask us to learn the history of a place before we call it home and
to consider the ways our fear might make
it hard for others to feel safe.

While this is the last chapter in this
book, it is not the last chapter in the
story of the neighborhood that shaped
a city. As this book goes to press, the
Central District is buzzing with coura-
geous, creative experiments in reclama-
tion and repair. Art, culture, belonging,
innovation, solidarity, and ownership
are everywhere you look, if you're paying attention. Many of the people driving those projects have stories and/or art
that appear in this book. Their memories of this place are in here; their dreams
for the future of this place are out there,
happening, right now. This chapter is the
in-between place; the grief for what was
lost and the memory that anchors everything to come.

Jill Freidberg

DURING THE '90s

in the early days of gentrification, people started moving into the neighborhood who didn't want to talk to anybody. They were calling the police on kids who were playing "That's My Car," a game where little kids will see a car, and maybe they'll go up to it and say, "That's my car."

It was a group of fairly small boys, seven, eight, nine years old. Short, little kids. They were all kids from the neighborhood. They were clustering around a late-model car and admiring it.

Without coming outside to ask the kids what they were doing, this person called the police. A guy who had just moved into the neighborhood.

There were a lot of things like that in that period, like the time my dad was scraping paint off my folks' house that was built in 1910. And the phone rings.

My brother answers the phone.

One of these block watch phone tree people was saying, "Oh, Mr. Mumford, I just think you should know there's a Black man outside banging on your house."

And my brother said, "That is Mr. Mumford."

That conversation ended quickly.
I wish I had been there to answer the phone.

Zola Mumford

THERE WERE A LOT OF

mom-and-pops and lots of small clubs. The 410 Supper Club, the Black and Tan, Pink Pussycat. We always went in groups, and if I wasn't with my husband, at least my family was there. When you added nieces and nephews, at one time, there was probably forty or fifty of us that lived in the Central District. Not anymore. Now I don't go places, because I don't have a relative to go with. I have a sister in Bremerton, sister in Everett, sister out close to Renton. We're all apart. I haven't been able to become close or very involved with new neighbors. I see them out walking their dogs. Well, no one wants to go walking with an old lady.

Narvella Jackson

AT CHRISTMAS TIME,

I would take each of my neighbors sweet potato pies. But now the atmosphere is so different. People pass right by our house. We like to sit out on the porch in the summertime and they pass right by. We the only Black people on that block now. My neighbor was a Black lady that stayed behind us, in this great big house, but she got sick. She had twelve children. When she passed away, they lost the house. I hated that so bad. Because she lived there before I did, and I lived there fifty-one years.

It ain't friendly anymore. People that walk the dogs right by, if I'm standing out there, they won't even speak. The little corner grocery store, where I live, is a dog shop now. I'm thinking, "Everybody got a dog!"

Lottie Cross

PEOPLE WERE SEGREGATED HERE

They couldn't live anyplace else. And they built this into a fine community. They were law-abiding citizens who raised beautiful children. They didn't make a lot of money, but they were frugal, and they bought these houses. They did the very best they could with their lives, and that's the story of the descendants of the stolen ones in every city; don't make as much money as everybody else, have more obstacles, have to fight for an education for their children, and they continue every day to walk out the door into a world that hates Blackness.

Harriett Walden

IN THE MORNINGS,

across the street, maybe about ten people would be waiting for the bus. All Black, you know. I'd go across the street and chat with them.

In the mornings now, I look over and there's no Blacks at all at that bus stop.

The sick thing now is that thing across the street, everybody in the neighborhood hates what happened with that. There was a nice little cottage there. We knew the family. The mother still owned the house, but her husband got sick, and they needed funds. The developers got to her. And we didn't know it. Nobody in the neighborhood knew that she had sold to a developer. I think she got 300,000 dollars. Developer built three townhomes there. 1.7 mil each.

Al Doggett

I THINK THE PART THAT HURTS

the most is to feel like the minority and to be treated as if we're not supposed to be here. To know that this is where you grew up, and this is where you've been all your life, and now people look at you like you're the stranger? People have asked me if I'm lost. "No, I'm not lost. Are you lost? Do you know what used to be here before you moved here?" So, no, we aren't lost, we're exactly where we're supposed to be.

Marie Kidhe

WHEN I WAS YOUNGER,

me and my parents and my grandma, my uncle, and then a few of my cousins, lived right in the Central District. Almost every Sunday, Seahawks game and then a big dinner. Grandma comes over, uncles, cousins. Family lived in multiple places around the neighborhood, so I can tell you like six different houses that we all had Sunday dinner in. It was cool because I could see my cousins whenever I wanted to. They would come over all the time, and we would just hang out. Everything was in a close proximity.

A lot of my extended family moved further south as house prices started to go up. It's just gotten harder and harder to see other family members. As far as all my cousins, it's so hard to see them now because everyone's spread out.

Sky Sawyer

THE CENTRAL AREA,

as we know, was redlined. It's the only place that African Americans could live for a very long time, and the care and love that came with that residency is evident. It's not a wasteland. It's a very well cared for community. Geographically, aesthetically, and that came from African Americans, Asians, all of the people who could only live in this area

Vivian Phillips

THE PEOPLE WHO LIVED HERE

didn't leave here by choice. They were pushed out.

Things first started changing when I was six. Our landlords changed. This white lady started to run our apartments. She'd walk around and wave her American flag at all the residents. She was so mean. Slowly but surely she started raising the rent on everybody, and there would be times when she would call ICE, and a lot of my friends were undocumented. So it was really unsafe for a lot of folks and they started leaving. By 2012, everyone was gone, there was new management, and the white lady sold the apartments to some really hipster-ass business who gave it a new fresh paint job and made it neon yellow.

My apartment's gone, my friends are gone, my family's gone. The places I used to kick it at are not the same.

My childhood feels like it's closed, really.

Aretha Basu

MY MOM WAS A SINGLE PARENT,

and her economic reality was paycheck to paycheck.

Now my mother lives with me, and our economic reality is that we can't afford to live in the Central, even though I have a good job. I couldn't afford to stay here because I have both my nephews that are living with me as well.

I knew that the housing crisis was bad, but somewhere I didn't stay in the loop as far as knowing how really bad it is in the Central Area. I'm thinking that it's gonna be easy to find something, and I'm looking online, I'm thinking, "This is a joke! Oh my god!"

And then, not just the reality of how much rent was, but the racism! I would call and make an inquiry about a house, and we would have been communicating by email, and then you get on the phone and the whole tone changes. I remember one time, I was asking about a house that was up there on 23rd and Union, very cordial over email, and then when we get on the phone, she hesitates, "I'll call you back." Never get a call back. You know it exists, you've heard the stories, but when it actually is happening to you, it was so horrible. It was so horrible.

KL Shannon

WHEN I FIRST CAME HERE,

this was a very loving community, and it was always a neighborhood where, while you walk down the street, people would say, "Hi, how you doing?"

Since that time? The neighborhood's completely changed. I mean, maybe when I take my grandson into Earl's Barber Shop, I'll see some people that are from the old neighborhood, but other than that, I rarely see anyone.

Just about everybody has moved out of the area because it's just too expensive to live here, really. Every once in a while, there will be a neighbor that will introduce themselves. Sometimes you go down the street and no one speaks to you at all. And I always, whenever I go down the street, "Hi!" Whoever. I don't care who it is, I speak to them and greet them. Sometimes people just walk on by. And it doesn't feel real good.

It feels lonely, very lonely.

Vicky Garner

JITE AGBRO
Untitled

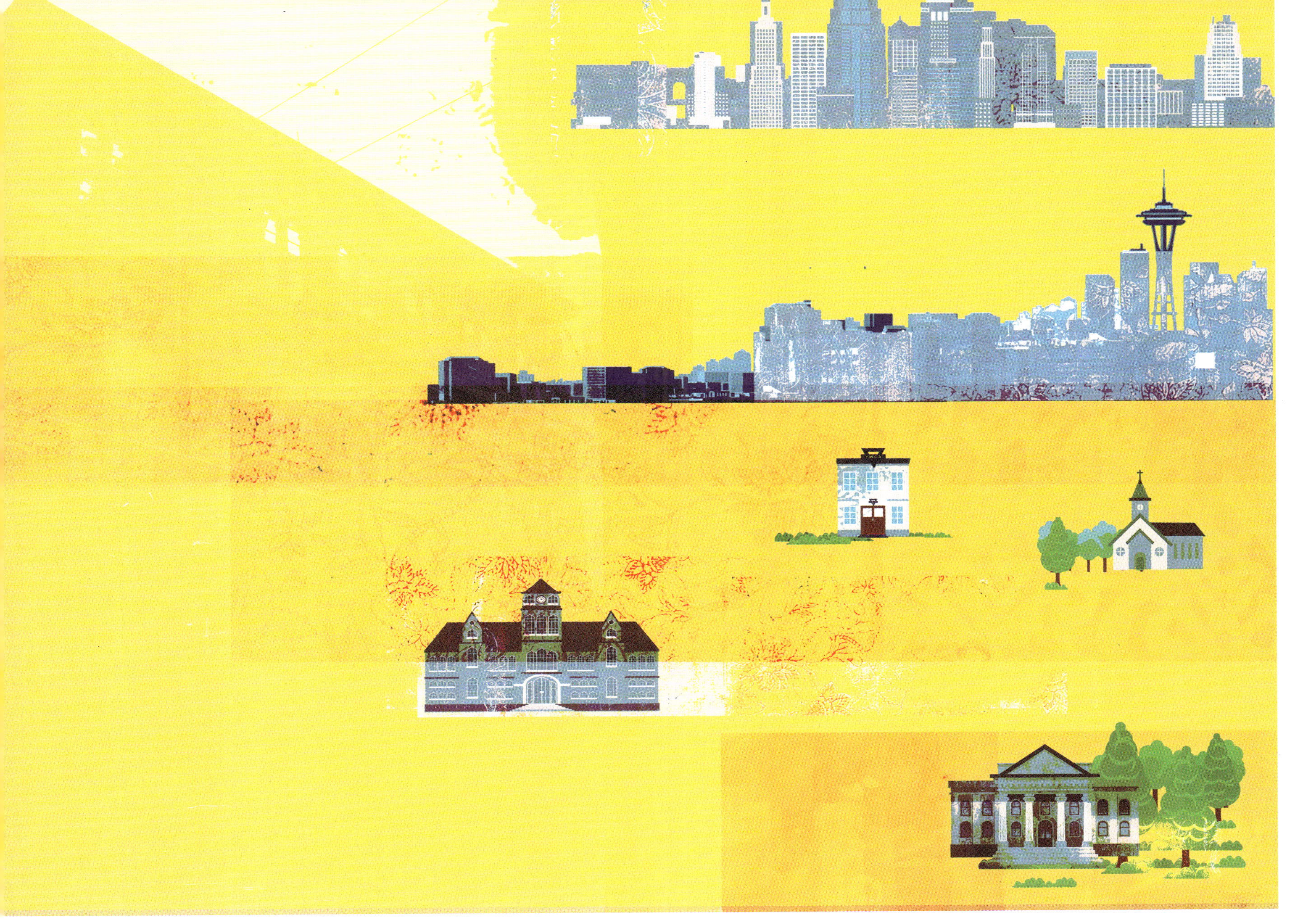

178: Robert L. Scott in booth at KYAC radio station, Seattle, May 1975; Courtesy Museum of History & Industry, Seattle (2002.68.1386.20)

181: Robert L. Scott in booth at KYAC radio station, Seattle, May 1975; Courtesy Museum of History & Industry, Seattle (2002.68.1386.16)

Back cover: Two servicemen sitting at a bar, Seattle, ca. 1945; Courtesy Museum of History & Industry, Seattle (2014.49.16.095.03)

Shelf Life interviews were conducted by Mayowa Aina, Domonique Meeks, Jill Freidberg, Rachel Kessler, Luvetra Miles, Chieko Phillips, Leilani Lewis, Henry Luke, and Sara Post

ARTIST BIOS

JITE AGBRO is a Nigerian American artist based in Seattle, WA. She is best known for her colorful figurative artwork that are comprised of layered patterns, textures and high contrast. Her work explores how people protect themselves using non-verbal communication, exchanging shared cultural, historical, and familial cues and ideas for the purpose of belonging and security. Jite is currently represented by Patricia Rovzar Gallery in Seattle, WA.

DAMON BROWN AKA Creative Lou:
I am a Seattle, WA based artist who, from an early age, knew I loved art and to create new designs. I drew inspiration from comic books as I spent countless hours exploring different images and heroic storylines which opened my eyes to artistic creation. As my imagination grew, I began to study various art movements, illustration styles, and urban art. This, in turn, taught to me how things like color, shape, story, and texture can manifest into something so vivid for people to feel and see. I was then able to blend my love for classical art and illustration.

Originating from Mindanao, the Philippines—a multi-ethnic, multi-faith island—**ROMSON REGARDE BUSTILLO**'s family immigrated to Seattle in the late '70s, joining relatives already rooted there as a result of the Philippines' colonial history with the United States. Raised in South Seattle and the Central District, Bustillo grew up in historically Black, immigrant, and working-class communities shaped by redlining and later impacted by gentrification. This layered cultural foundation, along with extensive travels across the U.S., Southeast Asia, Latin America, Europe, and Africa, informs his artistic practice. Romson is a recipient of the Seattle Print Arts Larry Sommers Fellowship (2016), the Garboil Grant (2017)—an award that considers artists "… engaging audiences outside the aesthetic industrial complex.", the Artist Trust Fellowship (2019), and the Artist Trust Artist Innovator Award (2021). His work has been supported by 4Culture, Jack Straw Cultural Center, the Glass Museum, and Pilchuck Glass School.

BONNIE HOPPER was born and raised in Seattle, Washington and is one of thirteen children. She studied art in the advertising art program at Seattle Community. Although art has always played an important role in Bonnie's life, she did not pursue her dream of becoming a professional artist until 2008 when she was commissioned to do a portrait by a friend of the family. In 2016, Bonnie began her association with Onyx Fine Arts Collective in Seattle, taking part in the "Truth B Told" exhibition for artists of African descent at the King Street Station, and was a selected finalist in Gallery 110's Emerging Artist Program exhibition.

Other accomplishments include shows at Harborview Medical Center in Seattle (2014), Renton Technical College in Renton, Washington (2018), Museum of History & Industry (MOHAl) in Seattle in celebration of Black History

Month (2022), Magnuson Park Gallery, showcasing thirty-two original works (2022).

INYE WOKOMA is a multi-disciplinary artist, journalist, and executive co-director of Wa Na Wari, a Seattle-based Black arts organization. His work explores personal narratives through the lens of politics, economics, and collective histories. For the past fifteen years he has explored the displacement of the Black community from Seattle's Central District, where he was born and raised. In 2019 he extended his practice to include the co-founding of Wa Na Wari, a social practice art project that transformed a Black-owned home into a center for Black art and community building. Over the past 15 years Inye has explored his own family stories through a socio-political lens. His contribution to the Shelf Life book invited him to reverse that process. The stories in this volume inspired him to create a series of photographic collages that merge imagery of social and political events with Pacific Northwest landscapes to present more meditative reflection on Black life in Seattle. Inye received his B.A. degree in journalism and filmmaking from Clark Atlanta University. He received 2002 Editorial Photography Award and a 2006 Photo Essay Award from the Society of Professional Journalists Western Washington, a 2004 National Council on Crime and Delinquency PASS Award for criminal justice reportage, a 2012 Telly Award for his film "Lost and (Puget) Sound", a 2019 Americans For the Arts Public Art Year In Review Award as a part of the groups show "Borderlands" and a 2019 Neddy Award Winner in the Open Medium category.

ERIN SHIGAKI is a fourth-generation Japanese American. She creates art that is community-based and often grounded in the World War II incarceration of her people. She is passionate about highlighting similarities between that history and systemic injustices communities of color continue to face. Erin's activism includes work on the annual Minidoka Pilgrimage to the American concentration camp where her family was incarcerated and with Tsuru for Solidarity, a nonviolent, abolitionist project of social justice advocates.

She is the recipient of grants and commissions from ArtsWA, the Wing Luke Museum, Densho, 4Culture, Seattle Office of Arts & Culture, National Academy of Design, and the Warhol Foundation for the Visual Arts, among others. She holds a B.A. from Yale University and believes that wielding art and activism can educate, redress, and incrementally heal.

CHI MOSCOU-JACKSON is an artist from Seattle, Washington. He studied in Toronto, Canada, at Ontario College of Art and Design. Chi's practice pursues mixed media and installation art. His work focuses on social, political, and current events and ecological themes. Collage is an important element in the creation of his work, mixing elements of photography, printmaking, sculpture, and drawing. Chi graduated, in 2013, with a BFA and minor in sustainable design.

Chin Music Press
1501 Pike Place #329
Seattle, WA 98101-1542
www.chinmusicpress.com

Printed in Canada

Library of Congress Control Number: 2025939030
ISBN: 978-1-63405-085-2

Editor: Jill Freidberg
Assistant Story Editor and
Research Assistant: Ariel Paine
Designer: Alison Keefe
Typeset in Merriweather and BAYARD

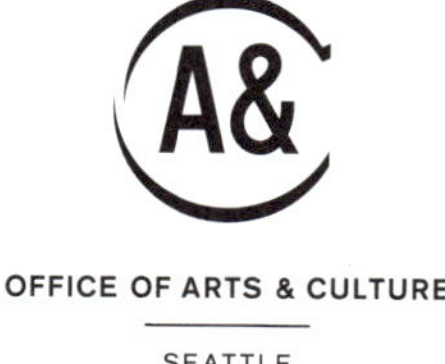

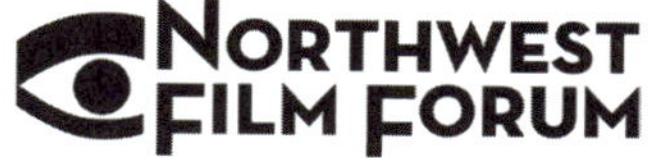

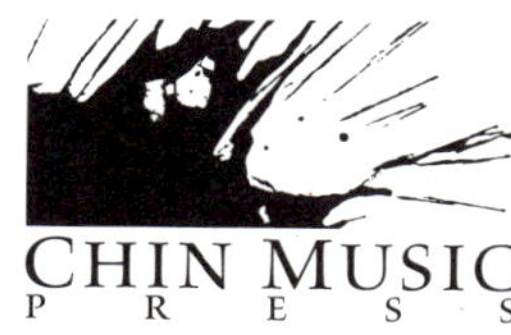

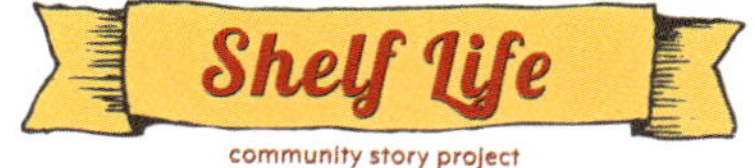